STUDENT PLANNED ACQUISITION OF REQUIRED KNOWLEDGE

The Instructional Design Library

Volume 35

STUDENT PLANNED ACQUISITION
OF REQUIRED KNOWLEDGE

Margaret Norton
Arlington High School
Riverside, California

William C. Bozeman
Division of Educational Administration
University of Iowa, Iowa City

Gerald Nadler
Department of Industrial Engineering
University of Wisconsin-Madison

Danny G. Langdon
Series Editor

Educational Technology Publications
Englewood Cliffs, New Jersey 07632

Library of Congress Cataloging in Publication Data

Norton, Margaret.
    Student planned acquisition of required
knowledge.

    (The Instructional design library; v. 35)
    Bibliography: p.
    1. Individualized instruction. 2. Problem
solving. 3. Creative thinking (Education)
4. Motivation in education. I. Bozeman,
William C., joint author. II. Nadler, Gerald,
joint author. III. Title. IV. Series: Instructional design library; v. 35.
LB1031.N66   371.39'4   79-23442
ISBN 0-87778-155-9

Printed in the United States of America.

Library of Congress Catalog Card Number:
79-23442.

International Standard Book Number:
0-87778-155-9.

First Printing: March, 1980.

FOREWORD

It is not often that one comes upon an instructional design which purports to require little in the way of development effort prior to implementation. Then again, few designs are so "process"-oriented that development takes place, in large part, *while* it is being implemented. Such would appear to be the case with the SPARK design.

As you read this book, you will come to appreciate three points which the authors have painstakingly explained in their communication of this instructional design. First, the personal experience of a teacher who has implemented SPARK is given. This helps us to understand what is required and the problems to be faced in trying this particular design. Second, SPARK itself is based on a generalizable problem-solving model (called PTR: Purposes-Target-Results), which has been successfully applied to other than purely learning needs. SPARK is one of the few designs that can boast this claim. Third, SPARK is a well-conceived, organized, and flexible system which can help meet an often-illusive need in education. This need relates to designs that not only assist in producing learning, but which also motivate students because *they* play a large part in the formulation and implementation of that design. The authors are to be congratulated for explaining and showing us how to make students a central part of the learning experience.

As a final comment, I think it particularly noteworthy to point out that you will find this design does not require additional instructional resources. It can work with one teacher in one classroom, and with what already exists in that classroom. The teacher need only understand and implement the design to see the results. (Of course, even more benefits can be derived from the design when collaboration with other teachers and additional resources are used.)

Danny G. Langdon
Series Editor

PREFACE

The instructional design concepts presented in this book are the fruition of an intensive course on a system design approach (now called the PTR approach: Purposes-Target-Results) sponsored by the National Institute of Education in 1972. The course, directed by Gerald Nadler, hosted 25 educators from throughout the nation, including the other authors of this book, Margaret Norton and William C. Bozeman.

Two course follow-up sessions provided the opportunity for the wide variety of education professionals to review their utilization of the PTR approach. A dean of education at a major university developed a registration system; a district superintendent reported how he handled an antagonistic football booster club meeting after he fired a winning coach; a dean of humanities resolved many difficulties with a curriculum design committee; a district superintendent and federal projects director used the strategy to secure proposal fundings; a high school principal developed seminars in his home state for administrators and teachers; and a director of instruction in a school district developed a drug abuse program for parents and students. These were only a few of the resulting projects which substantiated the utility of the PTR approach to planning, design, and improvement in education.

Student Planned Acquisition of Required Knowledge (SPARK) developed from the work of Margaret Norton subsequent to her participation in the PTR course and return to her junior high school teaching responsibilities. This book will trace Margaret's development of SPARK and her specific applications of PTR, as well as the general design concepts which are represented.

Although the principal concern of this book is the application of the PTR approach by Margaret Norton, it is appropriate to note a few of the varied and interesting applications of PTR by Bozeman and Nadler.

William C. Bozeman, in his work as a federal projects director of a school district and as a high school principal, found opportunities for numerous applications of PTR. These included project proposal development, design of compensatory and remediation programs, school activity planning, elementary and secondary curriculum design, and task force management. He also directed a number of PTR training programs for educational administrators, teachers, and instructional support personnel. As a university faculty member, Bozeman incorporates PTR into his courses concerned with educational systems analysis and design.

Many of the concepts and strategies employed within PTR are the product of the work of Gerald Nadler. Although the roots of PTR can be traced to engineering, Nadler has demonstrated, and continues to demonstrate, the efficacy and utility of this approach to many other projects and areas. A complete list of these applications would require many pages to enumerate, but included are programs of health care delivery, organizational management, information systems, work design, manufacturing and product design, and research and development of programs of individualized secondary schooling. As a university professor, Nadler teaches the PTR concepts to both his engineering students and students in the social sciences.

In one sense, this book represents a guide to SPARK and the general concepts of PTR. In a larger sense, it represents some of our answers to how the education establishment can "turn itself around" in achieving the goals so frequently voiced by its spokespeople. As an illustration, *Curriculum Change Toward the 21st Century* (Shane, 1977) notes that "(1) we are entering a period of great discontinuity and change and (2) mankind will be forced to find ways of adapting to increased interdependence of events, people, and nations in the coming decades." These lead to an explication and updating of the longstanding "Seven Cardinal Principles of Education" as goals for providing "the best preparation for effective living": (1) health, (2) command of fundamental processes, (3) worthy home membership, (4) vocation, (5) civic education, (6) worthy use of leisure, and (7) ethical character.

The report then goes on to propose some premises that interrelate the two points about the future and these goals. Although almost all would appear to be aided by the PTR and SPARK ideas presented here, the following seem particularly germane: "Education should take on a much broader meaning than formal schooling, and, thus, learning opportunities should be available in a variety of settings with a variety of mentors. Because learning and education are lifelong processes, learners of all ages, the very young through the very old, should be provided opportunities to learn. Progress through the educational process should be guided by the learner's abilities, motivations, and readiness rather than by birthdates and grade levels. Interdisciplinary learning and problem-solving approaches should characterize the acquisition of knowledge and skills. Learners should be taught the concept of alternative futures, and the skills necessary to promote the development of desirable futures."

We hope to show that these premises are significantly accomplished by utilizing PTR and SPARK. Reforming education with these approaches should move us a great way toward encouraging "the development of process skills, interdisciplinary learning, flexible learning modes, and a measure of self-directed learning" (Shane, 1977).

Many people continue to help in the development of SPARK and its related utilization in education. Among those from whose papers and applications we have borrowed, with many thanks, are Kathy Koritzinsky, J.V. Schultz, P.W. Struve, and J.C. Thomson, Jr. Others have encouraged us with words of wisdom and counsel, and those we recall for whom heartfelt thanks are sent include Sylvia Andreatta, W.P. Gephart, and R.A. Rossmiller. Several people are already acknowledged in this book for their reports of applications. Quotations, illustrations, and descriptions about PTR are used with permission from G. Nadler, *The Planning and Design Professions: An Operational Theory* (all rights reserved). Danny G. Langdon and Educational Technology Publications are due our appreciation for their foresight in suggesting this book be prepared and for their help in editing and publishing. And, to the many now anonymous students who thrilled us with their results through SPARK, we extend our deepest gratitude, for they are the real authors of this book.

M.N.
W.C.B.
G.N.

References

Nalder, G. *The Planning and Design Professions: An Operational Theory.* Draft version, University of Wisconsin, Madison, 1979.

Shane, H.G. *Curriculum Change Toward the 21st Century.* Washington, D.C.: National Education Association, 1977.

CONTENTS

ABSTRACT

STUDENT PLANNED ACQUISITION
OF REQUIRED KNOWLEDGE

This book presents an approach to instructional design and individualized schooling known as SPARK (Student Planned Acquisition of Required Knowledge). Though the primary focus of the book is the development of programs of individualized instruction through the use of SPARK, the concepts employed may be applicable to a wide variety of educational planning and problem-solving situations by both teachers and administrators.

SPARK is based on a generalized planning, design, and problem-solving approach known as PTR (Purposes-Target-Results). PTR has been widely and successfully employed in many fields for several years. Applications may be found in business and industry, health care, architecture, urban and regional planning, and engineering, as well as education.

This book includes the theoretical dimension of SPARK as well as actual examples of applications from classroom situations. Emphasized are the ways this approach leads to (a) creative thinking and motivation on the part of the students; (b) the involvement of students in assuming responsibility for planning and carrying out their work in the classroom; (c) an awareness of learning processes as well as subject matter; and (d) interaction between student and teacher. Other values of SPARK are: (a) it may be implemented by one teacher, a department, or the entire school; (b) it does not involve additional expenditures or physical resources; and (c) it is truly adaptable to individual student needs and abilities.

By using this design, students know why they are learning, what methods may be used to learn, and what the final outcomes of learning should be. They also learn PTR, a planning method which they may use in areas of their lives other than school. They can, in fact, learn a planning tool that will be useful to them throughout their lives.

STUDENT PLANNED ACQUISITION
OF REQUIRED KNOWLEDGE

I.

USE

There is no dearth of literature concerning the individualization of education. Only a glance at the journals and texts of the past decade will reveal a myriad of different approaches, programs, modules, packages, units, and products which claim to achieve this goal. Although many of these practices have become institutionalized in schools, many more have fallen by the wayside after only a brief utilization. Notwithstanding the efforts devoted to research and development of programs of individualized education, dollars expended for materials and training, and activities related to implementation, there are no guarantors of success.

Student Planned Acquisition of Required Knowledge (SPARK) also includes no guarantors of success. It is posited, however, that the likelihood of favorable implementation and utilization results is considerably enhanced due to the nature (e.g., emphasis on student learning) and uniqueness (e.g., students are motivated by their own design) of the approach. SPARK is an alternative to the more conventional programs of individualization which have been evidenced in recent years.

Most current models for individualized education incorporate methods for enrichment or acceleration. In these two models, there are activities and tests through which the student moves sequentially. In enrichment programs, every student spends the same amount of time in learning, and individual variability is evidenced in normally distributed test scores on unit and posttest criteria that correlate with measures of aptitude and environment. Acceleration ideally means that the criterion is fixed and time spent by each student varies (Walberg, 1975). Extensive research and development have produced programs, such as Individually Guided Education (IGE), Program for Learning in Accordance with Needs (PLAN), Individualized Design for Educational Activities (IDEA), and Individually Prescribed Instruction (IPI), as alternatives to traditional schooling.

Approaches to individualization, such as IGE, become quite complex due to the requisite organizational structure, curricular products, and system of components. For example, IGE includes components such as a multiunit school organization with various levels, an instructional programming model, evaluative procedures, curriculum materials, and a program for home-school-community relations. Clearly, such an approach is not embarked on by a school without much deliberation.

Such a system of individualized education is not only complex in design but also complex to administer and operate. Often, specialized instructional materials are required which are compatible with the precepts of the program. Instructional support personnel (e.g., aides, paraprofessionals) may also be required.

The management and record-keeping functions associated with programs of individualization may often become burdensome and quite time-consuming. This has led to the development of various computer-based instructional support systems or computer-managed instruction systems, such as WIS-SIM, PLAN, TRACER, and others.

Though the reasons which contribute to unsuccessful implementations of individualized programs of education are too numerous and complex to address in detail, there is reason to assume factors associated with failure may include:

- lack of teacher commitment;
- inadequate district support;
- insufficient training and preparation;
- little, if any, teacher involvement in program development;
- complex organization restructure;
- excessive costs;
- requisite record-keeping and clerical tasks;
- students are engaged in the program only as receivers of information (emphasis on instruction, not student learning); and
- programmatic arrangements depend solely on the present level of student motivation to make progress (difficult to motivate students not already so oriented).

The development of a program which will address the concept of individualized learning, while minimizing the likelihood of occurrence of the above factors, led to the development of SPARK. SPARK focuses educational activities on the student as a unique human being—not a statistical abstraction. SPARK allows for consideration of the many variables which may contribute to one's individual differences—the backgrounds, characteristics, goals, and requirements that are not common or shared with others. SPARK utilizes the well-established psychological finding that an individual is far more likely to change his or her behavior if involved in developing the expected pattern or solution. Even though SPARK is an alternative to the more conventional programs of individualization, it may, however, encompass many of the elements associated with current innovations in individualization, such as grouping of students for instruction, multi-disciplinary learning, optimal use of materials and facilities, and student time scheduling.

SPARK is an approach to the individualization of student learning. This approach consists of five basic components:

- a strategy or planning method;
- a solution framework which provides structure for the elements and dimensions which need to be considered and interrelated;
- a set of techniques for use by the individual or for involving groups of people;
- a teacher's role that is facilitative and based on knowledge of the resources, not authoritative, fixed, and superior; and
- a control method that lets the students monitor and correct their own performance.

Because a hallmark of SPARK is *process,* as opposed to utilization of some well-defined and highly structured program, the personal interaction between teacher and student becomes not only important, but essential. The student becomes involved in planning his or her own studies—not only what will be studied, but how it will be done. After all, each student has a different learning style. The student participates in a realistic fashion. Participation is not simply a goal in a curriculum guide.

An underlying assumption of the strategy employed in SPARK is that students learn, not only through activities which are presented to them by the teacher, but also through the planning and design of these learning activities.

SPARK encourages the use of community materials and resources. Friends, libraries, companies, churches, newspapers, colleges and universities, family members, government personnel—all these and many others have been used when SPARK is applied, and a teacher finds it easy to get students to use them when the student can do his or her own planning. SPARK thus fosters a great deal of creativity on the part of students.

An intrinsic value of this approach is the placement of a portion of the responsibility associated with planning with the student. There is a growing body of evidence showing that this may contribute to the effectiveness of the plans and the success of the design. Stated another way, the student is not only responsible for learning, but also planning how he or she will go about the process of learning.

By learning about and using an established process of planning and design, the student is also able to improve achievement in future education and in the world of work. SPARK is based on recent developments that show the approach to effective planning and design is different from the conventional research approach. The student is thus equipped with another method of problem-solving to help in future life activities.

Because SPARK is based on a planning approach, it may be utilized with a wide variety of curricular products in many disciplines. It does not require extensive purchase of new materials, comprehension of advanced technology, or major restructuring of the classroom or school organization. Record-keeping is greatly reduced because students do most of it themselves. In addition, there is so much verbal interaction between student and teacher that extensive records aren't necessary. Also, the teacher gives the students right at the beginning of SPARK what is expected in terms of criteria for evaluation, thus eliminating uncertainties and releasing students' thought processes for creative ends.

Though many of the examples presented in the following chapters refer to language arts applications, SPARK appears flexible enough to be employed in many areas of study—reading, mathematics, social studies, science, or the arts, including music, visual arts, and general humanities.

The processes and techniques employed in SPARK may be utilized in a dual fashion. Not only may they be employed by the student in planning learning activities, but also they have considerable value to teachers or groups of teachers in their design of various approaches to instruction. All too often, much time is spent unproductively in personal or group efforts to establish classroom procedures, organizational structures, whole curricula or curriculum units, or policy formation. SPARK embodies a set of guidelines and principles which facilitate all phases of planning. They stimulate creativity in such a way that effective results are realized.

What SPARK does, then, is to overcome many of the factors that may be associated with the failure of current programs of individualization. Characteristics of SPARK are compared with those of typical programs of individualized instruction below:

SPARK	Typical Individualization
Teachers employ SPARK only when the concept is deemed useful and appropriate.	Program must be employed in a manner consistent with its design; usage often may not be interrupted.
Teachers, on their own, can use SPARK with whatever resources are available.	Considerable resources are required, necessitating district support.
Teachers can learn SPARK on their own.	Extensive training and preparation is a requisite component.
Teachers develop their own program.	Little teacher involvement in program developments.
No reorganization is required.	Complex organizational restructure.
Minimal or no cost (perhaps some inservice training).	Increased monetary outlays.
Minimal record-keeping.	Increased record-keeping and clerical tasks.
Student learning is the focus.	Focus on instructional program and methods.
Student motivation and creativity are enhanced.	Motivation may not be given direct consideration.

Thus far, SPARK has been used with students to do their own planning in grades seven through twelve. Student teachers have also used it with students at these levels, as well as in grades five and six. It has been used with students of all ability levels. It has been used with classes in basic skills and with classes at the college preparatory level. It has been used in classes with either heterogeneous or homogeneous groupings. University of California-Riverside education department members, who attended a workshop conducted by Margaret Norton, have used it within their own department. Any group of adults should be able to use the ideas.

Some limitations on the applicability of SPARK exist in the instruction of groups of students with learning difficulties, as the process may become time-consuming. Although the strategies will still work, the teacher must balance time spent against the enthusiasm and effort generated in these students by helping them plan their own work. Another limitation, related only to the direct use of SPARK with students, concerns the minimum of four to five weeks it requires for a unit or topic. A typical sequence in a nine-week quarter uses the first week to introduce the subject, the second to apply SPARK in doing the planning, the third through seventh in doing the project according to the SPARK plan, and the eighth and ninth for presentations.

Summary

SPARK is a process approach for planning and design of learning activities suited for the individual. The nature of the technique employed in planning permits applicability to a wide range of instructional areas, levels, and disciplines within the curriculum. SPARK may be used by the student in the design of his or her own activities or may be used by individual teachers or groups of teachers. Individualization of learning and enhancement of overall effectiveness are achieved through:

- focus on the student as an individual;
- student/teacher interaction;
- student responsibility for planning;
- student learning and creativity enhancement through the process of planning;
- increased productivity of group efforts;
- usability with a wide variety of existing curricular products; and
- little or no additional demands on school resources.

Reference

Walberg, H.J. Psychological Theories of Educational Individualization. In Harriet Talmadge (Ed.), *Systems of Individualized Education.* Berkeley, California: McCutchan Publishing Corporation, 1975.

II.

OPERATIONAL DESCRIPTION

Student Planned Acquisition of Required Knowledge (SPARK) is based upon the assumptions, precepts, and research related to a planning and design approach known as PTR, or Purposes-Target-Results (Nadler, 1979). The PTR approach to planning/design/improvement differs from conventional strategies in several aspects, such as the phases or sequence of steps, the solution grid or framework employed, techniques for involving people, and a continuing change and improvement program. Examples of productive applications are both wide and varied in such diverse fields as engineering, management, industry, health systems, and education at all levels.

The best introduction and overview of how SPARK may be used in the individualization of learning is to follow along with Margaret Norton in her pioneering developmental effort and to illustrate how a specific student used SPARK. Chapter III, on "Design Format," will then explain the functional parts of SPARK that this chapter illustrates, along with other examples of PTR applications from a variety of settings.

Margaret Norton's developmental use of SPARK occurred in a series of steps that is useful to anyone planning to employ this method of implementing classroom instruction. When she first became interested in it, she was department chairman and a classroom teacher of English at a junior high

11

school. The school was centrally located in a middle-sized city in California. The students were of three major groups, "Anglo," Black, and Mexican-American. Many of the students from all ethnic groups were in the lower economic range. Many of the students had reading or learning difficulties, although there were also gifted students attending the school. Margaret was looking for a method which would allow students to be able to make more decisions about their own learning processes and to become more involved with their own learning.

Planning by the Teacher for the First Time

Individualization of instruction for each student is an objective extolled by educators at all levels. The rationale is axiomatic—each student is unique, has particular interests, learns in a unitary fashion, and develops at a singular rate. "Individualized learning" is the term we will use because it expresses the subtle, but crucially larger purpose of a focus of concern on the student, rather than on only the teacher's actions. Because success at achieving this purpose is so rarely obtained, Margaret felt PTR might overcome many obstacles that cause major disappointment in individualization of instruction.

Margaret's first introduction to PTR was through a conference and training program in 1972. At that time, she was introduced to the concepts and obtained practice using the planned approach in a variety of ways. Given this introduction, Margaret began to experiment with applications of the strategy and instructional planning.

For the person using this book, the *first activity,* after learning the basic concepts and formats, would be a series of individual practices in developing small plans, not all of which need necessarily relate to education. For example, plans for "an office filing system," "one day's lesson plan," "a one-day conference on composition instruction," or "a classroom discipline system." This practice will develop familiarity with the technique and confidence in the overall strategy.

The *next activity* is the introduction of the PTR approach to students in the classroom. The following pages show the steps in this process.

Margaret decided that the most effective use of the PTR approach in her language arts classes would lead to each student's design of his or her own study plans for each unit. Initially, students were scheduled to do their own development of study plans by the fourth or fifth week in the school year. This became impossible due to the large number of introductory topics presented at the beginning of the year. In addition, Margaret was applying the approach for the first time, with the usual fits and starts attendant to doing something new. The timeline that Margaret set up for herself did start introducing some of the ideas, such as purpose/function, fairly early. What actually occurred is summarized by Margaret as follows:

Margaret Norton's Description of Her First-Time Planning
Week-by-Week Summary

Week 1 School redtape and classroom organization. Activities for teacher and students to become acquainted with one another.

Week 2 Introduce the term *function.* Use it in a purpose/function expansion for "Classroom Water System." The students suggested many good purposes and functions for a water system in the classroom. Discussion of term *function* continued, since no one out of 185 students suggested that a function (probably the primary function) would be to provide water. This confusion on the students' part led to a good look at the purpose hierarchy.

Week 3 Students working in small groups tried to design systems to meet the purpose, HAVE WATER TO MEET STUDENT NEEDS. Most groups came up with little creative thinking. A few showed some imagination. Perhaps the best involved a condenser on the roof of the portable classroom to be powered by solar energy. Most groups expected a quick, one-paragraph answer without detail. They suggested buying bottled water, for instance, without considering cost factors, physical environment, etc.

Week 4 Discussion and evaluation of systems continued in class.

Week 5 I went through a period of discouragement and reassessment.

Week 6 About the only way in which the project development continued during this time was through my own use of the PTR approach in planning instruction. I did, however, call the attention of the students to the purpose of each lesson or unit of work.

Week 7 I attended the two-day follow-up workshop in Madison (October, 1972). Here I received help and some excellent ideas to implement upon my return to school. (The *third activity* the reader should consider is using PTR to design a unit of instruction. At this point, student involvement is mostly observation and analysis of what the teacher has produced in planning.)

Week 8 During week four, we had started some reading to correlate with social studies. U.S. history, exploration, and the colonial period were taught in social studies. The English classes were reading *Light in the Forest,* by Conrad Richter. This was the unit of work for which I had been designing a system. Upon my return from Madison, I had the classes do a purpose/function development for reading *Light in the Forest.* We discussed the directions in which study plans for this novel might move (e.g., to understand historical fiction genre, to understand the author's development of character). We examined the purpose/function hierarchy that I had been using (see Figure 1). The hierarchy in Figure 1 starts with "read book," the smallest scope purpose of the *Light in the Forest* Study Plan. The purpose of the function "read book" is to "know what happens in book." Each level thus expresses the purpose of the smaller scope levels. The hierarchy allows the most effective level to be the focus of efforts and puts the selected level into its context of larger purposes/functions. The level was selected to fit the conditions (time available, interest, resources, etc.). Then, we discussed the *sequence* that had been used in studying *Light in the Forest* (see Figure 2). (Figure 2 illustrates the use of the solution framework or grid.)

Week 9 Students turned in work that had developed from their own planning of what to read and what follow-up of reading to perform. This activity had been part of the sequence of the *Light in the Forest* Study Plan and gave students some structured practice in making decisions about what they wanted to do in class.

Figure 1

A Purpose/Function Hierarchy
Illustration for Students

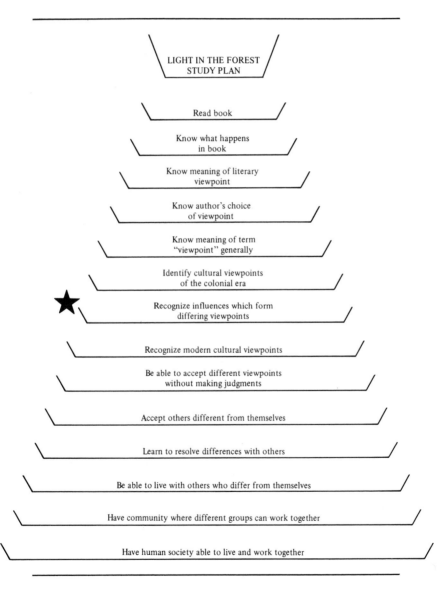

LIGHT IN THE FOREST
STUDY PLAN

Read book

Know what happens
in book

Know meaning of literary
viewpoint

Know author's choice
of viewpoint

Know meaning of term
"viewpoint" generally

Identify cultural viewpoints
of the colonial era

Recognize influences which form
differing viewpoints

Recognize modern cultural viewpoints

Be able to accept different viewpoints
without making judgments

Accept others different from themselves

Learn to resolve differences with others

Be able to live with others who differ from themselves

Have community where different groups can work together

Have human society able to live and work together

The three activities (practice, introduce PTR ideas, design a unit of instruction) for the teacher beginning to use PTR would probably take from nine to 18 weeks. The teacher should constantly practice the development of plans and use them during this period of time, so that confidence in their use is gained.

In developing and using this unit, I moved in the direction of gaining knowledge of use of the measures and control dimensions of the solution framework. It also had an important interface relationship with the units of work in the social studies classes. As one example, a film mentioning "Blue Jacket" was shown in social studies the week the book was being read and discussed in English classes.

This and the class examination of my purpose hierarchy and sequence elements led directly to the *fourth activity,* student development of their own systems for the next unit of work.

At this time, I introduced students to the structured sheets and to any limitations which would be set on the planning; e.g., bibliography required, date due, etc., and allowed class time for work on the planning. Students will need much individual help especially the first time they try to plan. As students become experienced, they can complete more planning outside of class and do it much more quickly. The following narration details my experiences with this activity.

As the second quarter of the first school semester began, we moved in the direction of students developing their own systems. Social studies material had moved into the area of studying the Revolutionary War period. The English classes began to read *Johnny Tremain,* by Esther Forbes. The first step was the introduction of the book to the class and the beginning of the reading process. Students who had reading difficulties read along with dramatized tapes. Students who read more easily and swiftly completed the taping of the chapters which had not been completed.

Figure 2

Specification of "Light in the Forest" Study Plan

PURPOSE: To have students recognize influences which form differing viewpoints.

INPUTS: Middle school students
Mrs. Norton, Mr. Leichtenberg (expertise)

OUTPUTS: Students recognizing influences that form differing viewpoints. Class and individual reports and projects. Growth in language arts skills.

SEQUENCE:
1. Introduce book. Have students begin reading.
2. Use worksheet identifying main character and his point of view in first two chapters and contrast this with point of view of minor white soldier character.
3. Students continue reading. This continues throughout. I shall not repeat it in plan even though it is going on constantly.
4. Present overhead lesson on literary point of view (omniscient, first person, objective, etc.).
5. Students in small groups write in mode-of-discourse (James Moffett) doing short sketch using point of view identified as being used by Richter in *Light in the Forest.*
6. Students choose second book to read within the limitation that it deal with Indian life or colonial period.
7. Lesson on simile and metaphor. Play simile game using *Light in the Forest.*
8. Second worksheet identifying other characters, their points of view, and possible causes for the viewpoints.
9. Vocabulary list from first half of book.
10. Lesson symbolism. Use of *Light in the Forest* to identify.
11. Read "The Massacre at Wounded Knee" in Scholastic magazine, *Search.* Discussion of varying points of view and their impact in causing the massacre. Students would have preferred to believe this story was fiction.

(Continued on Next Page)

Figure 2 (Continued)

12. First vocabulary quiz. Give out vocabulary list for last half of book.
13. Several days of small-group work role-playing points of view of Pyramid Lake, Nevada, controversy (Indians, Reno, Lake Lahontan, Lake Tahoe).
14. Reviewing *Light in the Forest* for episodes in which True Son makes decisions, and identifying the cultural background and point of view which influence his decisions.
15. Second vocabulary quiz.
16. Read to class portions of biography of Blue Jacket, young white man adopted by his choice into Shawnee tribe in the family of Tecumseh. Reinforce study of Indian culture showing both value system of the society and how it affected action. Brief introduction to difference between biography and historical fiction. Compare incidents in Blue Jacket's life with episodes in *Light in the Forest*.
17. Students choose from "68 Ways to Present a Book Report," and turn in work contracts.
18. Students finish reading second book and prepare reports (plays, panel discussions, dioramas, book covers, etc.).
19. Final test on *Light in the Forest.* Open book and take home.
20. Final presentation of second book reports.

ENVIRONMENT: Central Junior High School Campus. City and branch libraries. Students' homes.

PHYSICAL CATALYSTS: Classrooms, chalkboard, chalk, eraser, paper, pencils, pens, books and magazines, crayons, butcher paper, overhead projector, tables, chairs, etc.

HUMAN AGENTS: Teachers, aides, city librarians, parents.

INFORMATION AIDS: Data about Pyramid Lake and Wounded Knee massacre. Lists of books available to read as second book. Verbal or written annotation of various books. IDEAL concepts. Background information on various Indian tribes.

The second step was to give each student a structure within which to work in making his or her own plan. Each student obtained three sheets as soon as his or her reading was done or nearly finished, as shown in Figures 3, 4, and 5. On each actual sheet, space for the students to work out answers was provided.

Figure 3

Worksheets (8½ x 11) Given to Students

PAGE 1
JOHNNY TREMAIN STUDY PLAN NAME ....

1. List as many possible functions (purposes) for studying *Johnny Tremain* as you can (20-30).

EXAMPLES: To read the whole book
            To know what happens in the story
            To know the main characters
            To learn about colonial life
            etc.

It took most of the students the first four weeks of the quarter (until the time of the Christmas vacation) to complete their reading and to get their study plans worked out. Some students had completed their planning, imple-

Figure 4

Worksheets (8½ x 11) Given to Students (Continued)

PAGE 2
JOHNNY TREMAIN STUDY PLAN NAME ....

2. Work out a function (purpose) hierarchy or expansion. List on the first line the most immediate unique function (given). On each succeeding line, list a higher or broader function or purpose. Ask yourself either or both of these questions, "Do this in order to do what?" or "What is the function or purpose of this?"

EXAMPLES: What is the purpose of reading the book? We know what happens in the book.

Know what happens in the book *in order to* know Johnny Tremain as a literary character.

(These questions were followed by a function expansion ladder.)

Put a ★ by the function level for which you think you will plan. Copy this function in space 1 on page 3.

Figure 5

Worksheets (8½ x 11) Given to Students (Continued)

PAGE 3

JOHNNY TREMAIN STUDY PLAN   NAME ....

3. By answering the following questions, you should be able to plan a course of study for this unit that will achieve the function or purpose you have chosen.

    1. What is your purpose in studying *Johnny Tremain*?

    2. What are you doing this to, in, or on?

    3. What is the end-result or what does the end-result look like?

    4. What steps are to be followed to get to the end-result?

    5. Where and under what conditions is this being done?

    6. What equipment and physical facilities are being used?

    7. Who is doing this and how?

    8. What information is needed to keep your plan operating properly?

mented their system, and handed in an end-product in this four-week period. These students were given freedom to design another system within the language arts function area and implement this one also before the end of the nine-week quarter.

Others completed and implemented their *Johnny Tremain* study plan in the nine-week period but did not have a chance to complete another plan. A few finished their design but did not complete the implementation of it. Out of 108 students involved in this planning, two merely completed work to the first level of the hierarchy (Figure 1)—they read the book. Two others did not complete their reading.

My role as the students really got going on this work fell into two main areas. First, I kept various possibilities in front of the group as they began their thinking about what they were going to plan. For instance, I presented an overhead projector lesson on the sources of bibliography and the distinction between primary and secondary source material. One student decided to look for primary materials dealing with Boston during the colonial period. He found and read much of two volumes of collections of letters, diaries, and articles written at that time. Interestingly enough, this student was given a linoleum block printing set for Christmas and re-wrote his entire study plan so that he could make use of this kit. However, his reading had added to his background information and he made this comment on his final product, "I chose a block print of an engraving because it interested me and, also, as I looked through the books about the Revolutionary War, it seemed to me as if they had done a great deal of engraving for newspapers, books, and leaflets. Apparently, they were used in a way similar to the way we use political cartoons today." Another time, I played Stan Freberg's satirical record, "Stan Freberg Presents the United States of America." After class discussion of satire and the way in which Freberg had used some of the same historical information which had been used in *Johnny Tremain* in historical fiction form, one group of students wrote their study plan with the function of writing satire and producing a tape of their own based on historical information. They spent a great deal of time at one student's home. The tape is good for humor and incorporation of historical information. When they played it for me, however, they were the first to be self-critical and decide that they had not been truly satirical. This self-evaluation appeared to me to be an important product of the PTR approach the students were using.

The second important aspect of my role during these nine weeks was to serve as an information source and advisor. I had many individual conferences with students as they were writing their study plans. The greatest difficulty came as they worked on the purpose hierarchy. I would have to ask the questions, "What is the purpose of this?" and "You are doing this in order to do what?" They also needed help in working with page 3 (Figure 5).

Students would make requests for material as they got into the implementation of their plans and discovered that the school library was inadequate in the areas they needed. I obtained some books for them at other libraries. Students who became interested in the newspaper printing background given in *Johnny Tremain* had replicas of newspapers of the time provided for them. I gave the district catalogue of audio-visual materials to one group of boys who wished to order films and filmstrips to use in their plan. Some students, who decided to work in the area of how an author shows character development, borrowed some of my teacher manuals and texts. For most of the students, doing this design was interesting and satisfying. A few found it extremely frustrating. These few expected that I would tell them what to do. Having to plan their own work was almost threatening for them.

I, personally, found it a very busy, but very exciting, way of working with students. For one thing, I did not have to react to "grouchy" students asking, "Why do we have to read this?" They were too busy finding their own purposes to try this negative approach. The variety of responses fascinated me. Students were working in the areas of character development, theme of the book, satire, point of view, historical background, biography, etc. The end-products were also interesting, although far too many students seemed at this time to visualize the only possible end-product as a written report.

Most students gasped a little when I looked at their purpose (function) statement and their sequence of activities and pointed out to them that when they had finished the sequence they had outlined, they were supposed to know whatever they had said they wished to know in their statement. Nonetheless, this made sense to them and after the first shock or realization of what they were committing themselves to was over, most of them went to work with great earnestness.

The following is a partial list of some of the possible *Johnny Tremain* study plan purpose statements which the students came up with:

- To learn about colonial life
- To compare colonial ways of living to present-day ways of living
- To learn more about Boston then
- To learn about Paul Revere
- To learn about the author
- To know why the war started
- To learn about the author's style of writing
- To learn about blacksmithing
- To learn about printing presses
- To learn about colonial silversmithing
- To learn about Sam Adams

- To learn about John Hancock
- To learn about hatred
- To learn about the differences in social status
- To learn of death
- To learn how the British felt about the Americans
- To know about apprenticeship
- To know the causes of the Revolutionary War
- To understand the theme of proper and improper pride
- To see different ways of speech

The following is a partial list of purposes for which the students chose to design their study plans:

- To learn how Johnny Tremain develops from childhood to maturity
- To know about colonial silversmithing
- To know about the English taxes and their effects
- To know how the Revolutionary War affects us today
- To understand how an author shows character
- To learn about the events which helped start the Revolutionary War
- To learn about the occupations of colonial days
- To trace the history of printing
- To know about Paul Revere
- To know the Tory point of view
- To learn about secret organizations
- To trace the history of the Whigs and Tories
- To know about witchcraft in colonial days

A *fifth activity* is further use and refinement of student use of PTR. This could include showing students further examples of unit planning, explaining to students how smaller systems fit into larger systems (see Figure 14), or working out interfaces between systems with students.

A few interesting things happened as the students completed the work on their plans. Two girls seeking background material as they composed a skit on the Tory point of view read Shaw's *The Devil's Disciple.* One girl working on the history of printing called the office of the city newspaper and arranged for a speaker to give a presentation on how the city newspaper is now being printed. She cleared dates with me and made all arrangements herself. Another girl prepared overhead transparencies on events leading up to the outbreak of the Revolutionary War and gave a presentation during an entire class period. The social studies teacher said when he saw her work that he wondered why she was doing all of this work now in English when she had done so little in social studies. I believe that her work developed in this manner because she was trying to achieve the purpose that she had specified in her own plan.

Other interesting things happened as students who had completed work on their *Johnny Tremain* study plans turned to other things. One student wrote a system for a one-day teaching unit on poetry. She chose a poem by e.e. cummings and two others written by another student and herself as the basic material for this lesson. She prepared overhead transparencies to use in her presentation.

Several students, somewhat to my surprise, wrote plans for systems of vocabulary development. These students did not come up with any particularly creative or imaginative system to attain their purposes of learning words to use in communication with others. One student chose a teaching lesson system on a short story that she liked. Two others developed systems for teaching a lesson on folk tales.

Several developed systems centered around special interests and hobbies. These usually ended up with "How to . . ." papers or another library report as one that was done with the purpose, "to trace the history of the Arabian horse." One group used the purpose, "to produce a skit based on contemporary junior high life." This developed into a sketch showing some insight into actions and motives of young people of this age. The skit was titled, "Love—Junior High Style."

Parenthetically, the work on SPARK in my classes has led to contacts with persons in the educational structure of my school district. I presented the PTR concepts to a group of top administrators in the district, two assistant superintendents, two principals, and two supervisors and consultants. The concepts met with much approval. One comment was that finally students were getting *involved* in the process. Another was that this looked like the perfect method to achieve goals that the district had been working toward for a number of years; namely, the involvement of staff in planning and the focus on the purpose of educational processes. The suggestion was made that I might conduct seminars or workshops in other schools or lead a session that had met to do some planning.

Within my own school, I have been so busy with my students' designs and planning that I merely mentioned the PTR approach in passing to my colleagues. The present reaction is that I had better get busy and let them in on the secret.

One other rather complete illustration should suffice in presenting an operational description of SPARK. Figure 6 shows one student's list of purposes for another required reading unit. Figure 7 shows what he did in constructing the purpose hierarchy, and notes the level he selected. Figure 8 shows the plan he developed using the form Margaret prepared for all students. Figure 9 shows the control dimension report required each week, along with those submitted by several other students to demonstrate the variety of projects and control statements.

Margaret has found that a few further pointers in presenting the system to students may make its implementation easier for both teacher and students.

First, it helps in the initial presentation when the students are going to prepare their own plans for the teacher to stress that they will be learning to use a process that is useful in planning more than a project for a certain class and may be used in many other activities and studies. It helps to point out to those students looking forward to college that many college freshmen fail because they cannot plan their time and work efficiently rather than because they find the work itself too difficult. Learning to use SPARK will give students going on to college a process they can use effectively. For other students, point out that using this system of planning in the business world will probably enhance their chances of success.

Second, the teacher should allow sufficient time in class to work on the hierarchy of purposes. Since the hierarchy requires logical thinking, it presents the greatest difficulty for students. The teacher must watch to see that students do not move from higher level purposes back to a lower level; i.e., from "To evaluate the influence of Lord Burghley on Elizabeth I" to "To learn about Burghley's early life." Obviously, information about Burghley's early life and rise to power must be understood first in order to evaluate his influence on Elizabeth, but students do not always perceive illogical placement of purposes without help. It helps the teacher in judging the purpose hierarchy to observe that if correctly thought out it moves from the literal levels of learning to more abstract levels.

Third, the teacher should encourage brainstorming, especially for possible outcomes. Students definitely limit themselves in this area. An example might be in teaching the humanities unit on Rome to suggest that someone's project might be to treat the whole class to a trip to Rome and Pompeii to study the area first-hand. After the class gasps with amazement, some of the students may then suggest solutions they might not otherwise have thought of, such as planning a class visit to the Getty Museum in California to see a replica of a Roman house found in Herculaneum or checking to find out if the traveling exhibit on Pompeii will come to a nearby museum and could be visited.

Fourth, as it becomes apparent that students are having difficulty with some aspect of the system, the teacher should generate more examples to help them.

Thus, it is evident that the teacher is constantly problem-solving while working with the PTR system and with the students.

Summary

This chapter includes illustrations of Margaret Norton's design approach which led to the development of SPARK. Following Margaret's work step-by-step is, perhaps, the best introduction to SPARK and the PTR (Purposes-Target-Results) concept which it employs. In addition to the general concept of instructional planning, the description outline demonstrates obstacles and problems which she encountered and how they were resolved.

Reference

Nadler, G. *The Planning and Design Professions: An Operational Theory.* Draft version, University of Wisconsin, Madison, 1979.

Figure 6

Case Illustration of SPARK

CONTEMPORARY LIFE STUDY UNIT   NAME ...**Ed Hammer**..................

STEP ONE: Decide on the topic for your study this quarter as, for example,
Ecology, Generation Gap, Drugs, Crime, Dissent or Conformity,
New Morality, The Family, Life Styles, Future Shock, Ethnic Problems, etc.

STEP TWO: List as many possible purposes for studying this topic as you can
possibly think of. You may do this as a group even though you
plan to do your study by yourself. Sometimes the ideas that other
people have will make it easier for you to think about what you are
going to do. Work out on *scratch paper* to start with.

1. To read *Dig U.S.A.*

2. To recognize differing viewpoints

3. To learn about alcohol

4. To see how an alcoholic lives

5. To understand how he/she feels being this way

6. To see how his/her family feels about him/her

7. To know if he/she respects himself/herself

8. To know if he/she is losing any friends

9. To know the type of friends he/she is making or already has

10. To learn how many different types of alcoholics there are

11. To learn how the different alcoholics live

12. To know how many other problems they have after they become alcoholics besides their drinking

13. To learn how they became alcoholics

14. To know what they're planning on doing about their problem – if anything

15. To find out what they like about drinking or what they did like about it

16. To know if they started drinking on their own or if someone encouraged them in the beginning

17. To talk to the people on the A.A. plan and ask them different questions about alcoholism to get their opinions

18. To learn how an alcoholic affects his/her family

Figure 7

Case Illustration of SPARK (Continued)

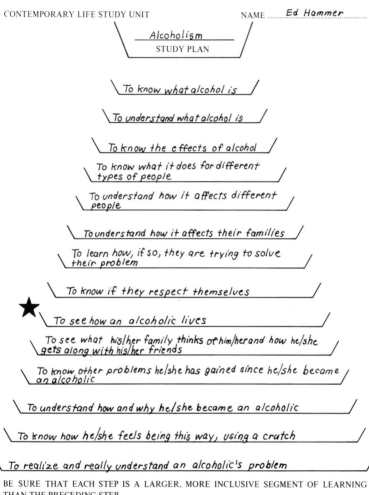

CONTEMPORARY LIFE STUDY UNIT   NAME .... *Ed Hammer* ....

Alcoholism
STUDY PLAN

To know what alcohol is

To understand what alcohol is

To know the effects of alcohol

To know what it does for different types of people

To understand how it affects different people

To understand how it affects their families

To learn how, if so, they are trying to solve their problem

To know if they respect themselves

To see how an alcoholic lives

To see what his/her family thinks of him/her and how he/she gets along with his/her friends

To know other problems he/she has gained since he/she became an alcoholic

To understand how and why he/she became an alcoholic

To know how he/she feels being this way, using a crutch

To realize and really understand an alcoholic's problem

BE SURE THAT EACH STEP IS A LARGER, MORE INCLUSIVE SEGMENT OF LEARNING THAN THE PRECEDING STEP.

BE SURE THAT YOU ALWAYS ASK YOURSELF AT EACH STEP, "What is the purpose of this?" or "Why do I want to know that?"

PUT A ★ BY THE PURPOSE LEVEL FOR WHICH YOU HAVE CHOSEN TO PLAN.

Figure 8a

Case Illustration of SPARK (Continued)

CONTEMPORARY LIFE STUDY UNIT – TOPIC ....*Alcoholism*........

	RATE	CONTROL
1. Purpose: *To see how an alcoholic lives*		*Self-control*
2. Input: *Me*		
3. Outputs: 1. *A Report on Alcoholism — Oral* 2. *Me — with knowledge*	*1 Report*	
4. Sequence (List steps to be followed in your plan to achieve purpose. List in order and in *detail*):		
1st week *Read a book about alcohol – The effects of it. Will get book Monday – 4/30/73* *I will take one week to gather material – written material from books, encyclopedias, magazines, etc. Any type of article. Will finish during the weekend.*	*1st week* *1 book, 1 encyclopedia. Look through 2 or 3 magazines. Any type of article about it*	*Check-Friday – of 1st week For Completion* *I changed from reading a book to seeing filmstrips*
2nd week Talk to different people about how alcohol affects them. Whether they are just a social drinker, a heavy drinker, or if they drink once in awhile. Will be entitled – Personal Effects and Feelings Toward Alcohol.	*2nd week* *Talk to 10 different people who drink heavy or light, including teenagers*	*Check-Friday – of 2nd week For Completion* *Wasn't completed until 5th week*
3rd week Take all of the material I have collected and organize it into different categories. Proofread. Organize for Oral Report.	*3rd week*	*Check-Friday – of 3rd week For Completion*
	For RATE, tell how many, how much, when items in column 1 will be worked on, learned, finished, etc.	For CONTROL, tell how you are judging progress and success of what you are doing and what changes you make to make plan work as you want.

Figure 8b

Case Illustration of SPARK (Continued)

CONTEMPORARY LIFE STUDY UNIT—TOPIC ...... *Alcoholism* ......

		RATE	CONTROL
4. Sequence (continued)			
	4th week Copy all material over. If happen to find something to add to my work, I will.	*4th week*	*Finish and Check For 4th week*
	5th week I will catch up on anything that I need to. I decided to do an Oral Report, so I also got a book called Alcohol and Youth.	*5th week Using a book Alcohol and Youth - And preparing for my Oral Report on Wednesday*	*Check - and will be finished Friday of 5th week*
5. Environment (What are the physical and psychological surroundings where you carry out plan?):	*In my room, in the school library, at school, in class, at home.*		
6. Physical Catalysts (What are tools, objects, materials used in plan? They do not change.):	*Pen, pencil, paper, people, book, an encyclopedia, a magazine, filmstrips with tapes.*		
7. Human Agents (Who will help you carry out your plan? teachers? aides? others?):	*Teachers, my mom, other students, and friends.*		
8. Information Aids (What must you find out in order to make plan work? a telephone number? an address? whether certain materials needed are available? etc.):	*I have to find out about Alcoholism. I need to get material for my report.*		

Figure 9

Case Illustration of SPARK (Continued)

CONTEMPORARY LIFE STUDY UNIT   NAME ....
CONTROL DIMENSION REPORT

Circle: Week 1 2 3 4   Date of report ....

1. What did you say you would get done this week?

2. What did you do this week?

3. What changes do you need to make to keep on target to finish work as planned?

SAMPLE STUDENT REPORTS
(transcribed exactly as written by students)

Mark, week 1, May 4
1. Read 2 books, cut out magazine picture to make poster, read paper every week, collect smog level
2. Due to heavy Soc. St and Alg homework only 3/4 of my first book was read, magazine pictures were cut out but lack of poster paper held it up, paper was read every day and smog level checked every day
3. Poster both done next week, faster reading on my books

Andy, Daryll, & Marcel, week 3, 5/17/73
1. Interview a conv. hospital's administrator
2. Tried to interview an administrator. When tried to make appointment but found that she wouldn't talk to us. So we went and talked to the head nurse, we found her to be helpful but not what we had really hoped for
3. None

(Continued on Next Page)

Figure 9 (Continued)

Rusty, week 1, Thursday
1. I was going to gather and read information I could get on how air pollution was affecting people and plants.
2. In the encyclopedia at home, I was trying to find something about it. I found one article about how mice die early from air pollution (they tested the mice with cigarettes). I also looked in our *Popular Science* book and found nothing much that helped me.
3. I need to gather a lot more information next week than I did last week, if I plan to make an outline for the 3rd week. I was going to go down to the smog research center this week where I planned on getting the majority of my information. It should tell a lot on how smog shortens lives, a little.

III.

DESIGN FORMAT

Obtaining the results Margaret describes is dependent on a wide variety of factors in addition to the SPARK ideas. Attitudes and capabilities of the teacher, climate for change and improvement in the school, and the concepts of planning and design practiced by the teacher and colleagues are among the most important. The latter factor, concepts of planning and design, is quite crucial for SPARK, and, as will be seen, can help significantly in improving the other factors, if they are not favorably disposed to producing the individualization SPARK seeks.

An understanding of what SPARK requires is enhanced by a review of the PTR planning and design concepts from which it emerged. A brief overview of the PTR approach will help the reader comprehend the nuances within SPARK that can make it effective in other settings. The first half of this chapter reviews the precepts of the PTR approach, while the second half explains how SPARK operates specifically by generalizing the illustrations of the previous chapter and providing additional examples.

The PTR Approach

Educators at all levels are frequently called upon to make decisions, formulate programs, effect curriculum changes or innovations, or simply to make improvements in their educational programs. At the classroom level, the teacher searches for a better way to achieve lesson objectives; principals, curriculum directors, and other educational leaders conduct meetings or direct task forces charged with developing or improving programs; and the district superintendent or his or her designee plans the system organizational hierarchy of authority and responsibility.

All of these educators share a common task—the improvement of the educational programs for which they are responsible. Inherent in this common task are two interrelated needs: the need for a general approach for attacking the improvement of programs, or, for want of a better descriptor, a "game plan" and the need for specific techniques or procedures; or, to maintain an analogy, "plays" that may be used to execute the game plan.

Our "game plan" is the PTR approach, and associated with PTR are "plays" which educators at many organizational levels and in many situations have found useful. The full "game plan" involves several major issues: (1) a strategy or pattern of reasoning or direction of thinking; (2) a solution framework that provides insight into what elements and dimensions need to be considered and interrelated; (3) a set of techniques for effectively involving individuals and groups of people; (4) a format for effective arrangements of organized knowledge, models, and techniques; and (5) a program of efforts to search for continuing change and improvement.

In general, the PTR approach is governed by several principles which provide guidance in the planning and design activities and capture a philosophy about change and improvement in a school. The PTR principles include both old and new ideas about getting the most effective implemented solutions, while utilizing most effectively the time and effort of resources allocated to the task. These principles are:

1. Treat each problem area in a holistic or system context, regardless of size.
2. Give people affected the *opportunity* to be involved in planning.
3. Each school and project are unique. Don't initiate a project by trying to install a solution from somewhere else.
4. Think *purpose*. Think purpose hierarchy. Continually ask *what* is to be accomplished.
5. Focus on what *should be* rather than on what presently is.
6. Develop *many alternatives* (as ideal as possible) before selecting one.
7. Develop a feasible ideal *target* for regularities (factors occurring most frequently or considered most important) to serve as a guide for continual changes.
8. Don't worry about everything at once. Treat *regularities* before irregularities. Separate activities which have different purposes.
9. Gather information only when necessary to answer a specific question.
10. Develop solutions that fit users (students, teachers, administrators, etc.). These are likely to be pluralistic and multi-channeled solutions.
11. Specify only the minimum number of critical details and controls. Give some flexibility to people operating the system.
12. Set up a schedule for *betterment planning* with PTR when implementing a solution.

The PTR strategy sets the stage for all of the other issues which follow.

Issue 1: Strategy.

What direction of thinking or set of actions should a group or individual follow in each of the major stages of planning along the timeline? The reasoning process of the PTR strategy can be summarized in five phases:

A. *Purpose Determination.* Develop a purpose hierarchy from which is selected the purpose/function the solution would achieve. Measures of effectiveness or conditions that will indicate successful achievement of purpose are identified for the selected level. They incorporate the outcome expectancies of those involved in the planning. In effect, this phase makes certain a purpose really needs to be achieved that will have a worthwhile "pay-off." It also avoids working on the wrong problem and allows proper prioritizing of various projects and functional components.

The major technique or "play" recommended for use in Phase A—to specify the purpose/function of the project—is purpose or function expansion. Initially, the individual or group develops as many purposes as possible for the problem. The many purposes are usually recorded on a flip-chart. From these possible purposes, the most specific purpose is selected and then is expanded to encompass other "bigger-level" purposes.

Expansion of purpose is accomplished by asking the question, "What is the immediate purpose of the given purpose?" By applying this question successively, levels of purpose are generated until a satisfactory purpose has been reached.

An example of such a hierarchy is shown in Figure 10. This hierarchy was developed by a group of high school students in the process of organizing their photography club. "To help gain photographic experience" was selected as the most specific on the list of possible purposes and was expanded into the hierarchy shown in Figure 10. The purpose "to develop photographic creativity" was chosen as the focus for the club.

B. *Solution Generation.* Generate creative and ideal solutions that achieve the selected and bigger purposes in the

Figure 10

Hierarchy Example

**Photography Club
Purpose Hierarchy**

To help gain photographic experience

To learn about photography

To gain knowledge about photography

To use knowledge about photography

To make good pictures

★ To develop photographic creativity

To express one's self

---

hierarchy. The basic "play" of this phase is brainstorming. An alternative which we recommend quite often is the Nominal Group Technique (Delbecq, Van de Ven, and Gustafson, 1975).

The Nominal Group Technique is applied by asking each group participant silently to write down ideas about how the selected purpose might be achieved. They are directed to write as many ideas as possible in five minutes. The group leader then asks one member at a time to supply an idea; the idea is recorded on a flip-chart exactly as presented by the participant. This round-robin procedure is continued until all ideas have been shared. Participants are encouraged to write down any new ideas which are suggested by the ideas being presented. No judgments are made about the merits of any idea.

Research has demonstrated that these procedures produce a large number of innovative ideas from a group while reducing the dominance of high-status, aggressive, or highly articulate persons. Because the technique is structured, maximum use is made of available time, often eliminating rambling and unproductive discourses.

An *ideal* solution has three characteristics:

   (a) it achieves the purposes desired effectively and innovatively;
   (b) it creates no new problems; and
   (c) it contains the seeds of its own continuing change and improvement.

Another form of describing this phase is shown in Figure 11. It compares the PTR strategy with the conventional approaches. The top of the triangle represents the ultimate ideal solution—one that costs nothing, consumes no time, and requires no resources. As one moves down the triangle, solutions become more ineffective and less ideal.

The intuitive approach is to try to make the existing situation better by solving a specific problem, that is, by moving up the triangle. The PTR strategy begins by looking at ideal ways to achieve the desired ends and *then* brings in the constraints of the problem as solution criteria; it starts at the top of the triangle and moves down as little as possible.

C. *Feasible Target Solution Development.* Group and shape ideas into major solutions from which a feasible ideal solution target is selected that considers only the regularity

Figure 11

The PTR vs. Conventional Solutions
for a Necessary Purpose

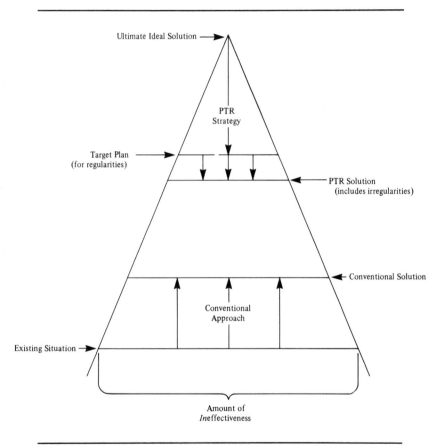

conditions (factors that occur with the greatest frequency or are considered most important). The target plan should be reasonably practical, but lacking sufficient detail for actual implementation. It is a solution for which to aim, a rough outline of the proposed solution. It does not include ways to handle the exceptions and problems that occur with any plan.

Many different "plays" are useful in this phase of the game plan. One technique that can often be used is the prioritization of the ideas generated in Phase B. A combination of the highest priority ideas can then form the target plan.

D. *Detail Recommended Plan.* Detail the workable solution or policy which incorporates all necessary irregularities and exceptions, while staying as close as possible to the target. Phase D activities can be most easily completed if a clear target plan has been outlined in Phase C. Without a target plan, planners often become confused and frustrated when they try to consider all details of a plan. They may become overwhelmed with too much information and retreat to standard and less satisfactory solutions. A target plan offers a convenient way to deal with one part of the plan at a time and avoid the frustration of dealing with too many details at once.

E. *Implementation.* Implement the workable solution, while letting purposes and the target guide all the minor decisions needed during implementation and in creating a continuing change and improvement syndrome. Included in this phase is evaluation and refinement of the solution, as well as determination, if the purpose(s) is really achieved.

Figure 12 illustrates how the five-phase strategy is put into practice. The first two phases open up the thinking and reasoning processes and encourage a focus on increasing the potential for an ideal solution. Only starting in Phase C is there some movement away from the creative and ideal potential by considering the real-world conditions.

Figure 12

Phases of the PTR Strategy

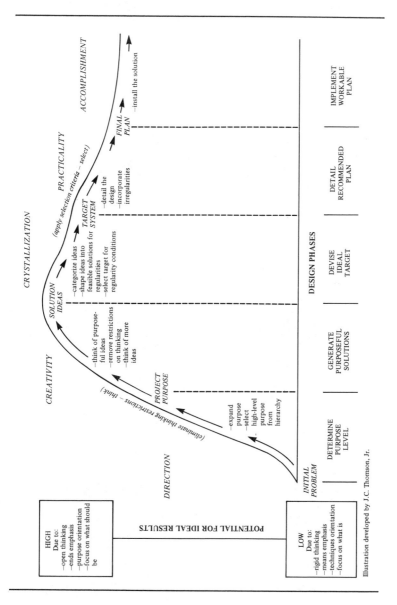

Illustration developed by J.C. Thomson, Jr.

Issue 2: Solution Framework.

A prescriptive structure is needed to guide the specification of a plan or policy. A framework of eight elements described in six dimensions is used in the PTR approach (see Figure 13). The eight elements carry fairly well-understood names: purpose, inputs (physical, human, and/or information items that become part of the outputs), outputs (desired and undesired), sequence or order of activities, physical and sociological environment, and items or agents (physical, human, and information) to aid in the sequence without becoming part of the outputs. The idea of dimensions recognizes that each element needs several properties and attributes and thus multiple forms of descriptions. The six dimensions are: fundamental characteristics, values (e.g., societal desires, motivating beliefs), measures (e.g., rates, objectives, goals, costs, etc., that reflect performance factors related to values), methods of controlling fundamental and measures dimension after the policy or solution is implemented, interface relationships with other systems, and future or planned state for the element.

The framework can also be considered a universal definition of the word *system*, posing the right questions as the strategy phases are followed. It provides a format for comprehensiveness and predictability, yet flexible enough to incorporate "soft" as well as "hard" decisions. The solution framework thus gives greater assurance that important considerations will not be omitted and that possible consequences can be assessed.

Issue 3: Role and Effective Involvement of People in Following the Strategy.

The role of a planner should be that of facilitator, catalyst, and coordinator, using the strategy and solution framework to stimulate often diverse people to generate *and* implement effective plan policies. This role does not release the planner

Figure 13

Solution Framework (System Matrix)

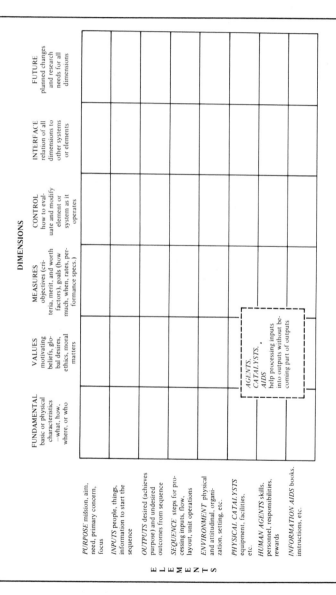

from knowing *when* to use the usual planning skills of measuring, modeling, and expert designing. Parents, users, citizens, experts, and decision-makers need to be included at appropriate times. New, effective group processes get currently involved personnel to take part as virtual equals, regardless of position, in a project team that follows the creative PTR strategy and generates willingness to accept and implement the results. The Nominal Group Technique, mentioned earlier, illustrates one of these newer tools.

Consider that the typical people who participate in seeking a solution are involved somehow with what exists, and thus know far more about it than analysts external to the situation could ever learn by applying *all* the techniques or by collecting lots of data. What's more, they know it in its context of interrelatedness, which is one reason why people can always find arguments against the usual analytical data—"accurate" factual data can never be the same as their overall knowledge. In addition, more people will take advantage of the *opportunity* (the crucial factor to continually offer) to participate when the strategy followed offers the challenge of purposes and creativity that foster the behavioral changes needed to implement solutions.

Issue 4: Format of the Knowledge Base.

Typically, organized knowledge about new products, processes, and research results is applied without real understanding of its use or necessity. It may be used because people just say that "data breeds solutions," or because the latest technology "ought to be" applied if the group is to be considered up-to-date.

With PTR, modern technologies, including systems analysis techniques, are applied and experts are utilized only as they are needed and appropriate. The PTR strategy identifies this need when it is followed on a project. In addition, the techniques are used primarily to prescribe solution conditions.

Know that a question has a real purpose before collecting information, calling in an expert, modeling it, or applying a technique. This is a way that technological advances can best become "a shaping force in education."

Issue 5: The Effort Committed to a Program of Continual Search for Change and Improvement.

Each teacher, school, or district should have a program of continual *search* for change even in a successful solution, perhaps at its very peak of success. Why wait until serious difficulties arise and people are then threatened?

An effective continuing change and improvement program treats a solution being implemented as "provisional," as a means of encouraging change, taking risks, and recognizing the need for continual planning. This creates an atmosphere where decision-makers and implementers are freer to search for change rather than where a given decision is assumed to *solve* a problem and there should be no further change.

Policies are needed to set up a continuing change and improvement program—how to generate interest in the program, where it should be located organizationally, what type and how much PTR education should be available, how to offer the opportunity for people to get involved, how project teams get established, what type of audit and review of the program ought there to be, when parts of the program should be implemented, and so on. Establishing specific continuing change and improvement program policies for a school is accomplished by following the PTR strategy with education personnel and a broader community.

This will produce a continuing change and improvement program that fits the uniqueness of the community or setting. Each situation requires its own program, rather than importing a structure and set of policies from somewhere else. Even effective programs elsewhere should be viewed only as data points of knowledge on which to draw when necessary. Success of a program elsewhere does little to predict its success in another setting.

The PTR approach utilizes and builds on large amounts of evidence that challenge continued adherence to the use of conventional or research-based approaches. Some of that evidence is:

1. People have been shown to be poor information aggregators, yet the research approach, when used for planning and design, immediately collects huge amounts of data. Who can possibly assimilate all of it? Information overload is serious in all settings.

2. Large amounts of information create conservatism in decision-making. The more a person digs into something, the less likely he or she is to change it or even find ideas that might change it.

3. Psychologists show that people will defend "their" system if they are confronted with statements that "prove" something is wrong with it. Isn't this exactly what analysis, subdivision, and gathering of facts do?

4. Functional fixedness is a well-defined psychological phenomenon. How is this overcome by in-depth review of what already exists?

5. Experiments with planners on real problems show that the research approach produced significantly less technical quality in results and took more time for equivalent quality results than a PTR approach.

6. The interacting discussions that characterize most group meetings polarize prediscussion tendencies and are much less creative and productive than the Nominal Group format.

7. Change theorists conceptualize three categories of principles operating along the timeline: (a) getting an organization, agency, community, etc., started, (b) the process of developing the specific changes, and (c) implementation of solutions (Savas, 1975). How much of a start can diagnosis and delving into what exists give in getting the

involved people to implement a change—especially when such analysis is urged upon the organization because the *analysts* want it for *their* consideration?

Such evidence as well as examples of successful applications illustrate some of the advantages and benefits of the PTR approach. Consider, for example, the essentiality of the purpose hierarchy. Anyone can identify and label a purpose, but knowing the context within which it fits is indispensable. A hierarchy is needed and can be approximated regardless of how big the initial project may appear. Note the advantages of focusing initially on purposes:

1. The probability is much higher that the correct problem (purpose) is selected, and that a great deal of the fear people have of "losing" is dissipated. This is the best type of problem—generation, identification, and formulation actually enable the problem to be treated as an opportunity. The hierarchy permits holistic thinking.

2. Even if full agreement on the hierarchy and selected purpose are not obtained, discussions take place in the positive direction of purposes. The process is far more likely than conventional approaches to achieve "good convergence." The appropriate purpose level is far more likely to be selected because the "solution space" is larger than the problem-as-stated. It gives people a chance to determine if thinking big is beneficial.

3. A context for any planning is well-established even if the purpose level that initiated the hierarchy is selected. The hierarchy gives continuing assurance of working on the right "problem."

4. Because the hierarchy starts with current perceptions of the problem, people are concurrently "expanded" in their understanding. Functional fixedness is less likely to occur.

5. The bigger-purpose levels are guides to developing creative solutions and serve as criteria to evaluate alternative ideas for solutions. It helps to pose the right questions.

As another benefit, consider the regularity concept. Everyone knows that complexity and variability surround any problem, but why assume that the idea generation phase must *at first* incorporate all the complexity? Everyone understands the regularity idea because they can mentally grasp and cope with one or two regularity conditions. Complexity doesn't overwhelm them. Combined with the purpose hierarchy, regularity is a key stimulus to being creative.

As still another advantage, the effective direction of thinking can help individuals in quite sensitive situations. Consider the plight of one superintendent of schools who fired a consistent *winning* coach in a rabid football district. (Sufficient reasons existed for the removal, as indicated by the complete agreement to the action by the board, athletic director, and athletic staff.) He was "invited" to a booster club meeting to explain why. Almost all of the 40 people who attended wanted to "nail the superintendent to the wall." This is the exact phrase used by the president of the club when he introduced the superintendent. The superintendent uses PTR in the district and did so at the meeting. In his words, "At the meeting, I started by asking them about the purposes of football and athletic programs. Then we discussed what is an ideal coach to meet those purposes. Through the whole meeting I never said one negative word about the coach because that would have created a defensive reaction from the rigged audience. But they really developed a pretty good list of purposes and then of the characteristics of an ideal coach, especially from a pretty negative group of people. From here on, the group did discuss the weaknesses of the current program, and developed a good idea of where to look for a new coach. And when I was finished, the meeting was over. No one asked, why did you fire the present coach? They answered the question themselves."

Consider also the benefit of how the PTR approach

effectively balances our multiplicity of preferences, interests, and goals. Many cases illustrate this through the effectiveness of results: better policies and solutions (as measured by whatever real-world criteria are important, such as reduction of time delays, increased quality, variety of work, lowered costs, and/or more service), increased integration of available knowledge and techniques, appropriate introduction of technology as needed rather than as made available, increased recognition of individual differences, greater chances for an innovative breakthrough in the problem, reduced time and cost necessary to complete each project, better growth and development of people, long-range planning potential through the hierarchy and target ideas, and greater commitment to "change is stability."

"Change is stability" is an advantage. It shows how the future can be explored systematically and continuously, rather than assuming that some futurist's snapshot is certainty. For example, one junior high school utilizing PTR developed a school-wide reading improvement program in which all teachers would be involved, and in addition, set up a PTR planning "system" for the school to do its own continuing planning of changes and improvements in the reading program and other projects.

As a final advantage, the five issues demonstrate the effectiveness of another approach for planning and design while retaining the research approach as most effective for developing laws, generalizations, and theories. It demonstrates the validity of having different approaches for the different purposeful activities of humans. It leads directly to the uniqueness of SPARK and how it came into being.

SPARK (Student Planned Acquisition of Required Knowledge)

As might be expected, SPARK is an approach to individualization that depends on ideas other than a set of modules, structure of committees, learning packages, and so on. It can include any, all, or more, of these conventional results of individualization product developments, but it depends on getting the student involved in the process of individualization as opposed to being only the recipient of individualization decisions of others. Figure 14 puts this idea into a purpose hierarchy which demonstrates that students not only develop their own study plans (levels 4 and 5), but also learn the difference noted above between an approach to planning and design and one to do research (level 8).

Several important needs in schools lead to the focus in this book on just the technique of SPARK rather than including all the various planning and design needs in education where PTR would be extremely useful. First, the direct learning activities of each specific student seem to be rather overlooked in the individualization literature. Students are treated in the aggregate or only superficially on an individual basis with data used in CMI or other records. Getting students involved in their own learning individualization needs a planning approach, such as that formalized in SPARK.

Second, tight budgets should not stop the adoption of advanced educational concepts, even though new equipment and packages or system-wide, school-wide, or curriculum changes and improvements are very likely to be ruled out. A crucial learning point still occurs at and is dependent on the teacher-student interaction. Much more should be expected at this point through low to no cost improvements.

Third, continuing benefits from individualized learning can be obtained, even though an overall individualization program is not put into effect, by concentrating on the direct teacher-student contacts of SPARK. Teachers can learn how to use the approach rather easily. It can also be used selectively in the classroom on some of the units or continuously on all the units. It can be expanded as much as possible to the curriculum, school, and district.

Figure 14

Purpose Hierarchy for Student Individualization

1. Have students learn basic skills

2. Have students learn advanced skills

3. Have students learn literary concepts

4. Have students initiate
reading-writing study programs

5. Have students do independent study and reading

6. Have students use knowledge in daily life

7. Have students share knowledge with others
(including planning, design, research, etc.)

8. Have students prepare for future life pattern

9. Have students become producers in society

Briefly, SPARK includes four general steps or phases:

1. Each unit of study (theme, topic, book, project, etc.) is presented to a class with any definite requirements.

2. Each student or group of students applies the purpose oriented planning strategy to the unit of study as a means of identifying his or her foci of interests that provide motivation for learning.

3. The teacher reviews the resulting detailed study plan with the student or group to assure that it fits within the framework provided by the topic and any requirements established by the teacher.

4. The student carries out his or her learning plans, including the control reporting agreed upon in the plan, with teachers and others acting as resource persons, information sources, and advisors.

Unit of Study and Requirements

Every course has certain requirements (book to use, items to read, projects to complete, etc.) established by the curriculum, school, district, and/or state. Each teacher also has optional units as well as discretion about most actual methods used in the classroom for all units. Although all units could be handled by SPARK, in the beginning it may be advisable to try two preliminary phases:

(a) Use the purpose oriented planning strategy in developing a specific syllabus for a particular unit of study. Then tell the students in detail *how* you followed the strategy in developing the teaching plan that you then follow in the classroom. Review what you did after the unit is over to refresh the students about the strategy and how you adapted actual class activities to meet the conditions while staying as close as possible to the teaching plan and purpose.

(b) Pick out *one* subsequent unit of study very soon afterwards on which you will have each student try out the strategy. Follow through to the end to give the students and yourself a chance to really learn it.

Although the initial theme or topic and specific requirements for a SPARK unit are selected by the teacher, selection may be made jointly by students and teachers in accordance with student interests and learning objectives after students become familiar with the process. Themes or topics may range in scope from basic skill mastery plans to specific content topics, such as poetry or chemical elements, to broad interdisciplinary themes, such as contemporary life styles or ecology.

The "Operational Description" chapter illustrates these ideas as Margaret followed them. *Key to successful utilization of SPARK is the planning of the teacher.* This cannot be overemphasized or repeated too often, for the teacher is crucial as a resource to the students in developing each individual study plan. Familiarity with the strategy and approach is but one part of the teacher's role. Sharing the utilization of the approach with its iterations and trials with the students overcomes the "perfection" syndrome of problem-solving so endemic in education.

In addition, the teacher learns how to follow the PTR approach in many other educational situations. Figure 15 illustrates how several teachers can interrelate various areas within the humanities to meet a common purpose.

Purpose Oriented Planning Strategy

The PTR strategy describes the thinking process, direction of actions, or steps followed by a student in the development of his or her learning plan. These are the same processes as those followed by the teacher. The thought process adapted for SPARK represents several unique features which are illustrated in the Ed Hammer case in the "Operational Description" chapter.

Purpose Determination. The student should begin the planning strategy by listing as many purposes for the required project as possible (within some time constraint specified by

Figure 15

*Interrelating Several Teachers' Areas
to Achieve Common Purposes*

Roman Literature System	Roman Architecture System	Roman Leaders System
Have students read selections		
Have students identify themes of selections		
Have students relate themes to Roman life		
Have students discover satire as Roman development	Discover relationship of buildings to values of Roman society	Decide what characteristics were Roman ideals for leaders
Have students learn how satire reflects Roman values		

Learn how literature, art, history, recreation, etc., reflect a society's values

Decide what the major values of Roman society were

Determine what Roman values seem to have universal appeal

Compare Roman values with present-day U.S. values

Decide which values should be encouraged

To encourage positive values

To avoid pitfalls and decline that met Romans

To have continuing U.S. civilization

the teacher). This can often provide a good exercise for small groups of students in a class. These purposes which relate to the assigned or required project should be topics, issues, or objectives that the student is interested in or ones that the student feels are "best" for him or her. This exercise helps alleviate the apparent arbitrary specification of objectives which students so often feel accompanies a plan of study. This step also introduces variety and an opportunity for creative thought.

After completing the list of possible purposes, the next phase involves generating a purpose hierarchy. From the initial list of purposes, the student selects the purpose which is smallest, narrowest, most unique, or which represents the most essential statement of purpose (for the project). Ideally, the selection should not represent the purpose of any other assignment This concept of the smallest or most unique purpose is difficult to describe and may be hard for students to comprehend at first. That is why the illustrations employ very explicit, observable, and even obvious purposes at the first level (e.g., to read . . ., to calculate . . ., to survey . . ., to know . . .).

This initial purpose is expanded to form the hierarchy which will encompass other "high-level" purposes. The expansion is accomplished by asking, "Why do I do this?" or "What is the (immediate) purpose of this?," for each purpose to find the next purpose.

Students are continually aided in the process by reviewing examples the teacher prepares in his or her utilization of PTR/SPARK while getting classes ready. Figure 16 shows a list of purposes a teacher gave her students when starting a Roman literature unit in humanities studies. It could be used in any unit, even though it is somewhat incomplete so that students are able to start their own thinking, not just copy the teacher's. A form similar to Figure 15 is also given to the students, but using only filled in examples of the left and

Figure 16

Example of Planning a Study List

HAND IN AT END OF PERIOD

TOPIC *Roman Literature*
1. Read Virgil's *Aeneid*
2. Learn names of Roman writers
3. Classify types of writing
4. Learn what satire is
5. Learn about epigrams
6. Identify major writers
7. Know how writers earned money
8. Know how books were produced
9. Find out what literature was taught in schools
10. Find out who Maecaenas was
11. Read writings of Horace
12. Read writings of Martial
13. Decide whether historical writings should be included as literature
14. Learn what an epic is
15. Compare the *Aeneid* and the *Iliad*
16. Know how books were used in libraries
17. Know whether writers were honored in society
18. Know topics that were written about
19. Identify major themes of writers
20. Decide how writers reflected personal feelings
21. Decide how writers reflected feelings of their society
22. Learn the history of Roman literature
23. Learn about the effect of translation on literature
24. Find out . . .
etc.

---

right small hierarchies. The middle hierarchy area is left blank for the students to fill in. It is these opportunities for the student to be creative, even within a well-defined requirement, that is most beneficial to SPARK. The teacher, in working with students while they develop their plans, thus is always able to stress and illustrate the interface between what the teacher designed for classroom instruction and what the student is planning to do individually.

A word of caution bears repeating. Care must be taken by the student (and the teacher or anyone else developing a plan) to focus on purposes in developing the hierarchy. An initial tendency of people is to put in the hierarchy what really belongs in the sequence of the solution framework (Figure 13). In other words, people may confuse *when* and *how* they learn with what they are seeking to accomplish by learning.

Purpose Level Selection. When the hierarchy is complete, a purpose level is selected as the focus of the project. Figure 7 illustrates Ed Hammer's hierarchy for his alcoholism study plan and his selected level. The purpose hierarchy allows the student to become personally and systematically involved in the determination of "why" he or she is studying a given topic or unit. This is a significant enhancement of the usual methods in which the topic objectives may appear somewhat arbitrary to the student. The hierarchical development of purposes also forces one to think beyond the more typical, immediate purposes of studying a topic. As a rule, our experience indicates that as the student moves toward his or her focus of study (i.e., bigger-level purpose), the teacher's purpose and/or study objectives for the class and respective students are also accomplished. This may be illustrated in the hierarchy in Figure 17.

The forms prepared for the students should fit the students with whom the teacher is working. Those used in Chapters II and III are quite simple and depend on the

Figure 17

A Student's Hierarchy Showing Relationship
with Teacher's Purpose (see Figure 15)

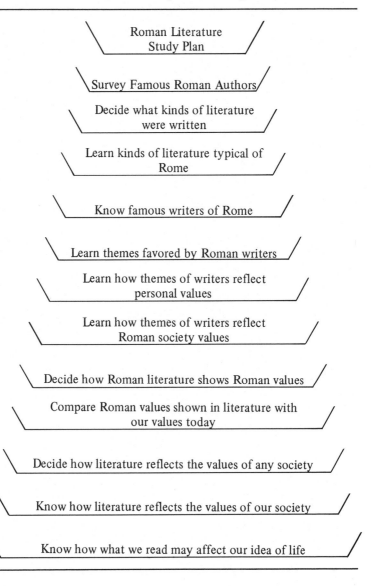

Roman Literature
Study Plan

Survey Famous Roman Authors

Decide what kinds of literature
were written

Learn kinds of literature typical of
Rome

Know famous writers of Rome

Learn themes favored by Roman writers

Learn how themes of writers reflect
personal values

Learn how themes of writers reflect
Roman society values

Decide how Roman literature shows Roman values

Compare Roman values shown in literature with
our values today

Decide how literature reflects the values of any society

Know how literature reflects the values of our society

Know how what we read may affect our idea of life

individual student understanding the process. For those who may have some difficulty, small revisions might help. A blank hierarchy form, for example, may be typed with "in order to" written at each level. This seems to help students who cannot think the question to themselves each time.

Dealing with purposes/functions, hierarchies, and selecting appropriate levels in one or more hierarchies permit teachers to cope with the critical interfacing between what one might think of as subject matter content and skills development. If a teacher has designed a system for classroom instruction using, for instance, the purpose, *to learn the relationships between Roman values and their literature, art, music, history, etc.,* the teacher can also design a system with the purpose, *to have students learn basic research skills,* and another with the purpose, *to have students learn several literary terms and genres.*

The teacher can then flesh out the interfacing between all three systems so that a lesson is designed focusing on satire which includes both a study of Roman life and the values of society with the satirist's criticism of certain values as well as work on the definition of satire and its history as a literary form. Another lesson might include a brief survey of Roman leaders with an exercise on correct note-taking skills using a variety of source materials. A third lesson might study the epigram as a literary form, and, by having students write their own epigrams, relate modern values to Roman values.

Notice how this really helps teachers who do not understand the trite but useful saying, "Every teacher should be a teacher of reading." By designing systems, first for covering content, and second, incorporating reading skills and then interfacing them, it becomes possible and easy to incorporate reading skills into subject matter disciplines.

Solution Generation. List possible ideal plans or solutions. What are the various ways that the selected purpose could be achieved? Many are available. The student is now not only allowed, but, in fact, is stimulated to use his or her creative abilities, because no idea on *how* to achieve the purpose is considered foolish at this point. The teacher acts as a resource to stimulate the student by pointing out many alternative learning routes that may not have been considered. Student motivation is increased because the selected purpose is now his or hers. As Margaret put it, "I did not have to react to grouchy students asking 'Why do we have to read this?' They were too busy finding their own purposes and ideas."

Students can be aided in generating innovative ideas for their study plans by having a stimulator list available, as shown in Figure 18. This is often a critical aid in utilizing SPARK. Many students reach high school apparently brainwashed into thinking they can only do a written report. One of a teacher's hardest tasks might well be to urge more creativity and variety in planning student projects.

Feasible Target Solution Development. Develop a target learning plan. The student groups his or her many ideas to form three to six relatively cohesive or major possible plans of action. Ideas that fit in several major plans should be included. Especially sought are innovative ideas and plans. The alternative cohesive plans are reviewed to select the one which is most feasible, yet innovative, for "regularity" conditions, or those which occur most often or are most important. A feasible target plan for regularities guides the development of a workable, implementable plan that incorporates exceptions and irregularities.

Again, the teacher helps the students formulate the alternative major possible plans and the criteria the students might consider in choosing the feasible target. Figure 8 shows Ed's target plan in a solution framework (or system matrix format) prepared by the teacher. Figure 19 shows another plan in a simple solution framework format for the Roman literature project.

Figure 18

Stimulator List

There are many ways to get your brain working and exploring possibilities for achieving your purpose that you might never have considered without help. Look at each individual item and let it spur or prod your brain. Each item can be used as a stimulus to suggest other possibilities to you. How could you transform any of these suggestions and use them to accomplish the purpose you selected?

miniature stage setting	speakers	diary
costume design	programmed instruction	myths, legends
movie	electronic teaching devices	proverbs
pantomime	punched cards	first editions
puppets	color coding	bibliography
dress up	sampling	speeches
outline	operating rules	persuasion
diorama	calendar	notebook
mural	dates	filmstrip
timeline	a day at . . .	catalog
crossword puzzle	". . . you were there."	mobiles
choral verse	executions	clay
radio script	newspapers	scissors
debate	archaeology	jigsaw puzzle
interview	cameras	paint
decoupage	crayons	boxes
editorial	phone calls	community
invitations	advertising poster	background music
tall tales	travel lecture	microfilm
collector's items	tape recording	scrap materials
mottoes	letters	leadership
original manuscripts	map or chart	manual of instructions
group trip	book review	learning capability
TV program	model	gossip session
point of view	paper dolls	religious services
file box	re-write	vendors
illustrations	songs	trials
club	plays	food, menus
collage	commentaries	cartoons
synonyms	panel discussion	epigrams
soap	public service	butcher paper
pliers	news story	typewriter
overhead transparencies	advertisement	videotape
felt tip pens	imaginary friends	

Figure 19

Roman Literature Study Plan

Purpose: To decide how Roman
          literature shows Roman
          values

Inputs: Mary Jones, Sam Brown,
          Susie Phillips

Outputs: 1. Ourselves & knowledge
          2. 8mm film to show class

Sequence:
  1. Read encyclopedia section on Roman liter-
     ature   Oct. 4
  2. Check out book, *Roman Literature in
     Translation*   Oct. 5
  3. Read above book   Oct. 7-14
  4. Choose which authors will be studied   Oct. 14
  5. Plan dramatization of one episode   Oct. 15-18
  6. On weekends, shoot film dramatization   Next two weekends
  7. Have film developed   by Nov. 2
  8. Preview film and do tape   Nov. 9-10
  9. Arrange with teachers for class presenta-
     tion   Nov. 11
 10. Bring tape, film, and projector for small
     groups   Nov. 16
 11.
 12.
 etc.

Environment: At home, school, Fairmont Park,
              by Lake Matthews

Physical Catalysts: Camera, film, tape

Human Agents: Parents, teachers, librarians,
                other friends

Information Aids: How long does it take to get film developed?

Teacher Review of Study Plans

Modifications in the target plan are made when necessary irregularity conditions are considered. As few modifications as possible are sought. Group activities for utilizing collective creativity are often used to help a student stay as close as possible to the target. The teacher serves again as a resource in helping the student find methods for staying close to his or her target plan. A workable recommended plan emerges for each student.

Although teacher review is listed as a separate phase of SPARK, it should be apparent by now that the teacher-student interaction through the process thus far both pushes the student to be innovative yet lets the plan be practical at this point, while achieving the purposes of both teacher and student. The review is thus an opportunity for the teacher to be sure each student is proceeding in an attainable direction.

Implementation and Control of Plan

Implementation of the recommended plan is quite straightforward because each student is motivated to do what *he or she* designed. Responsibility for individual action is fostered through the submission each week of "control dimension" reports (see Figure 9) by each student. Figure 9 also illustrates several actual reports.

Evaluation of the individual or group projects is facilitated by a three-part form with as many individual items as desired—achievement of teacher requirements (e.g., a bibliography is to be included), written presentation, and other presentations. Figure 20 illustrates a type of evaluation form. Distributing such forms to students informs them in advance of how and on what items they are being graded, at the same time not in any way inhibiting them in going in any direction they desire in selecting a purpose or choosing a plan of study action.

An effective summary of the design format for the

Figure 20

Project Evaluation Sheet

STUDENT .... PROJECT TITLE ....

I. WRITTEN
...... A. Project notes
...... B. Bibliography
...... C. Fulfillment of plan
...... D. Footnotes
...... E. Mechanics
...... F. A-V support
...... G. Organization of project
...... H. Quality and relevance of material
...... I. Quality of writing style

II. CLASS PRESENTATION
...... A. Project notes
...... B. Bibliography
...... C. Fulfillment of plan
...... D. Organization of information
...... E. A-V support
...... F. Organization of presentation
...... G. Quality of presentation, including technical effects
...... H. Quality and relevance of content
...... I. Special effects

THIS EVALUATION SHEET MUST BE TURNED IN AS THE FIRST PAGE IF YOU HAVE A WRITTEN PROJECT.

THIS EVALUATION SHEET MUST BE TURNED IN WITH YOUR PROJECT NOTES, BIBLIOGRAPHY, AND PLAN WHEN YOU MAKE A CLASS PRESENTATION.

---

students is shown by way of illustration in Figure 21. Both parts are obviously changeable to fit the circumstances, especially the special instructions on the second page and the topics on the third page. The list of suggested topics students may use is not meant to limit them to any of them. Some teachers feel more comfortable with this approach, which one of Margaret's student teachers uses.

Summary

An important dimension of SPARK is the planning and design strategy which it utilizes—especially as related to the PTR concept. The PTR approach incorporates a number of group/behavioral techniques and strategic models which may enhance the planning and design process. The essential component of the PTR may be demonstrated as five phases: (a) purpose determination, (b) solution generation, (c) feasible target solution development, (d) detail recommended plan, and (e) implementation. The solution format utilizes a prescriptive system definition for description of appropriate elements. Benefits of this approach include effective and efficient use of human and material resources, facilitation of change and implementation, and enhancement of overall quality and quality of results.

References

Delbecq, A., A. Van de Ven, and D. Gustafson. *Group Techniques for Program Planning: A Guide to Nominal Group and Delphi.* Chicago: Scott Foresman, 1975.

Savas, E.S. New Directions for Urban Analysis. *Interfaces,* 1975, *6,* 1-9.

Figure 21

Directions for Planning and Project Work

I. Do your plan following the instructions for each part.
  A. List of possible purposes
    1. Decide on the broad topic for your study. Check list of possible topics for help.
    2. List as many possible purposes for studying this topic as you can possibly think of. Try to think of all the possible things you could learn about this topic. You may do this in a group even though you plan to do your study by yourself. Sometimes the ideas that other people think of will help you to think about what you are planning.

      Examples: 1. To read one play by Christopher Marlowe
              2. To read a play by William Shakespeare
              3. To compare Marlowe's characters with Shakespeare's

  B. Purpose Hierarchy
    1. Use hierarchy chart. Check your example.
    2. Be sure to list your purposes starting with the smallest, most basic, possible idea, concept, or activity.
    3. Move step-by-step to larger, more inclusive segments of learning.
    4. AT EACH STEP ask yourself, "What is the purpose of this?" or "Why do I want to know that?" OR TELL YOURSELF, "I learned this in order to . . ."
    5. Put a ★ by the purpose level you have chosen to plan for. Enter this purpose in step one of part C.

  C. Planning
    1. Purpose: Enter starred purpose from hierarchy.
    2. Inputs: Enter name of one or ones who will learn.
    3. Outputs: 1. Enter names of learners + knowledge gained.
                 2. Enter work that will be done and handed in or presented (film, bulletin board display, overhead presentation, etc.).

(Continued on Next Page)

Figure 21 (Continued)

4. Sequence: Detail the steps that will be taken to carry out the work of learning. Too much rather than too little detail is needed. Be prepared to plan for things that may turn out to be hard to accomplish.
5. Environment: List when and under what conditions work will be done.
6. Physical Catalysts: List equipment and physical facilities being used (film, India ink, overhead projector, etc.).
7. Human Agents: List people who are helping you (a neighbor, a relative, a college librarian, etc.).
8. Information Aids: List items you need to keep the work going (a phone number, an address, etc.).

II. Special instructions:
  A. Limitations are given below.
    1. Only .... working on any one project.
    2. Project due date is ....
    3. You must have teacher approval of your topic.
    4. You must have a "B" or better on your study plan before starting work.
    5. Written projects must observe correct form: footnotes, etc. NO PLAGIARISM.
  B. Control sheets will be required each week.
  C. Consider alternatives.
    1. Don't settle on a written report without considering other ways of presenting your material.
    2. Think about how *you* learn best (orally, writing, drawing pictures, making models, etc.).

TOPICS FOR ELIZABETHAN AGE UNIT–HUMANITIES

Remember that these are broad, general topics. In your planning, you will be narrowing your actual topic to a small segment of the broad topic.

(Continued on Next Page)

Figure 21 (Continued)

Elizabeth I
Henry VIII
Globe Theater
William Shakespeare
Anne Boleyn
Christopher Marlowe
Elizabethan Life Styles
The Tower of London
Courtiers
Education
Mary, Queen of Scots
William Cecil, Lord Burghley
Sir Francis Drake
Robert Dudley, Lord Leicester
Sir Walter Raleigh
Holinshed
Hakluyt
Hawkins
Frobisher
Gilbert
Harriott
The Golden Hind
William Harvey
Edmund Spenser
Robert Devereux, Earl of Essex
Sir Francis Walsingham
Houses
Art
Architecture
Madrigals
Law

Sir Francis Bacon
Nicholas Hilliard
William Byrd
John Dowland
Ben Jonson
Dances
Musical Instruments
Foods
Commerce
Shipping
Travel
Recreation
Empire Expansion
Spanish Armada
Military Activities
The Navy
Shops
Guilds
Inns and Pubs
Printing
Textiles
Clothing
Cooking
Child Care
Medicine and Health
Superstitions
Religion
Lyric Poetry
Government
Universities
Privy Council

OTHERS: Can you list 20 other ideas?

IV.

OUTCOMES

Specifying the results of SPARK needs more than just a list of the "final" products students develop. Chapter II already described quite a few of these. The additional dimension required stems from the process or pattern of *thinking* inherent in SPARK. It is just as oriented to its utility for all types of planning and design activities (curriculum, school organization, district administration) as it is to the acquisition of specified knowledge, and more, by the student. *Learning* effectiveness and efficiency are the direct benefits and advantages to the student through SPARK; and other, often overlapping, values are also part of SPARK's outcome:

1. *Clears thinking.* A teacher using this approach can be sure of teaching material for which a definite learning purpose has been established. It helps the teacher to rethink what he or she may have been doing for years without questioning the usefulness and value of the activities. It encourages brainstorming and getting out of the rut of the same old thing year after year. Searching for the "ideal" way to implement instruction allows change to occur.

2. *Student involvement.* Students become involved in setting their own learning purposes and in planning and controlling their learning activities. They become responsible for their own instruction in part, rather than always being told or expecting to be told what to do by the teacher.

3. *Individual differences.* Since students are designing much of their own study, they can work within their own interests and capabilities. The use of the control column (see Figures 8, 9, and 13) allows flexibility to meet special needs. Gifted students can go as far as they wish in using their talents to the best advantage. Slower students can legitimately plan to do less and still succeed in carrying out their plans.

4. *Variety of methodology.* By choosing different purposes, a teacher or student can handle material in different ways. One example is a folklore unit which was originally taught as traditional classroom instruction. It was then restructured to meet the purpose, *to have students use Learning Activity Packets for individualized instruction.* It was restructured again with the purpose, *to have students work through Bloom's affective domain levels.* In other words, content, which remains rather constant in the three purposes, is handled very differently depending on the purposes used.

5. *Changes teacher-student roles.* The students develop far more initiative in planning their own work and come to regard the teacher as a helper and resource person rather than as a "dictator." The teacher has more opportunity to work with students on a one-to-one basis. More interest and excitement in learning are generated.

6. *Interface teacher requirements and student planning.* The teacher prepares the sheets of paper that the students use, and can include whatever purposes are desired for that unit. Evaluation sheets can be used as considered appropriate. Most important are the individually arranged, one-to-one reporting mechanisms and the resource role that the teacher now plays.

7. *Students realize that more than one approach to problem-solving is available.* Conventional problem-solving is based on analysis of existing conditions, which students learn is just fine when working on research problems. When

working on a planning problem, the SPARK (and thus the PTR) approach is more effective.

Outcomes can also be discussed on the broader level of education as a whole: The Preface reviewed some of the goals and premises of education for the 21st century. It becomes easier now to note how SPARK (and PTR) provides significant assistance in preparing students as well for their future lives. To reiterate some of the premises noted in the Preface:

- Learning opportunities should be available in a variety of settings with a variety of mentors.
- Learners of all ages, the very young through the very old, should be provided opportunities to learn.
- Progress through the educational process should be guided by the learner's abilities, motivations, and readiness.
- Interdisciplinary learning and problem-solving approaches should characterize the acquisition of knowledge and skills.
- Learners should be taught the concept of alternative futures, and the skills necessary to promote the development of desirable futures.
- Reforms should encourage "the development of process skills, interdisciplinary learning, flexible learning modes, and a measure of self-directed learning."

Lastly, an important outcome is, surprisingly, the lack of an either-or outcome. That is, SPARK is a process from which there is an almost infinite number of outcomes. The level of teacher involvement and commitment can be variable, the frequency of the use of SPARK can be variable, the type of student projects can be variable, and so on. The *change* in education that SPARK can bring about is not imposed on a teacher or school from the outside. Packaged management programs and one-shot inservice sessions are not the basis for improving student learning. Experienced teachers are able to use their vast backgrounds productively rather than having them assume their knowledge is somewhat obsolete. SPARK can thus avoid the condition recently noted in a RAND report (Berman and McLaughlin, 1978): "The number of years of teaching had negative effects; the longer a teacher had taught, the less likely was the project to achieve its goals or to improve student performance. Teachers with many years on the job were less likely to change their practice or continue using the project methods after the end of federal funding."

In other words, SPARK can continually improve the outcomes of the learning and educational processes without the stigma of any particular level being called "poor." Using it only once a semester is better than not using it at all, and trying to use it twice the next semester is still better. Even if three or four years elapse until it is used regularly, "success" is attained.

Reference

Berman, P., and M.W. McLaughlin. *Federal Programs Supporting Educational Change, Vol. VIII: Implementing and Sustaining Innovations.* Santa Monica, California: Rand Corporation, R-1589, May 1978.

V.

DEVELOPMENTAL GUIDE

An important characteristic of the Purposes-Target-Results (PTR) strategy employed in SPARK is the provision for using variations on the strategy rather than being forced to adhere to a rigidly-defined sequence of steps. It has been the experience of the authors, however, that it is helpful to follow the phases of the strategy closely at first, until the user becomes comfortable with the general format. Once this is accomplished, the many ways of using the design methods are only limited to one's imagination and ingenuity. This chapter presents a recommended guide for using SPARK following a step-by-step procedure. Remember to feel free to move about among these steps as the situation requires.

Phase One: Purpose Determination

1. Present the group or class with the selected unit of study. This may resemble the traditional classroom assignments, such as a book, a reading assignment, investigation of a topic, science experiment, group project, etc. The topic or unit of study should be reasonably well-defined by the teacher but should *not* include the format or procedures to be followed by the student. Given below are a few examples of assignments:
   —Properties and characteristics of magnets
   —Reading of a novel

—Behavior of a pendulum

—Organization of city government

—Preparation for a job interview

2. Have the student(s) develop a list of possible purposes/ functions related to the topic. These purposes should be brief, succinct statements. They should also be operational rather than abstract. Examples of possible purposes are:

   —To study magnetic properties of different metals

   —To explore applications of magnets

   —To learn how metals acquire magnetic properties

   —To determine strength of magnets at different distances

   —To develop empirical formulae related to magnetic bodies

   These examples of purposes incorporate a suggested format or style—that is, using an infinitive verb form followed by an object or objective phrase. It is important to make this list as complete as possible.

3. From the list of possible purposes developed by the respective members of the class, each student should select from his or her list the most specific, unique, or least-general statement. This statement should be relatively narrow and can be considered to lead to the other purposes. For example, the *purpose* statement, "to determine strength of magnets at different distances," is smaller and more specific than the purpose, "to develop empirical formulae related to magnetic bodies."

4. Given this selected purpose, a purpose hierarchy is developed. The purpose hierarchy is structured by asking the question, "What is the purpose/function of this?" This recognizes that every purpose/function must be part of and have a larger or broader purpose. This concept may be better understood by studying the examples in Chapter III.

5. Once the purpose hierarchy is carried to a quite large level

(and one shouldn't be concerned about carrying it to a very big level!), the student may select a purpose which seems most appropriate.

These five steps complete Phase One, the determination of the purpose/function of the project or study. Although, at first glance, much of this work may seem a trivial exercise, it may well constitute the single most important phase of instructional planning. The experience of the authors has demonstrated that the quality of a design is likely to be no better than the statement of purpose. Phase One may be presented schematically in a flowchart (see Figure 22).

Phase Two: Solution Generation

Activities associated with Phase Two, solution generation, are directed toward the design of a plan or system which will accomplish the selected purpose under ideal conditions. The student should list as many ideas as possible which will achieve the purpose. Remember—an *ideal solution* need not consider "practical" limitations, such as available technical or financial resources.

This phase is one in which the student has the opportunity to be creative. Initially, students will have a tendency to only offer solutions which resemble previous study options. Innovativeness and imagination must be encouraged and cultivated. *No* idea, regardless of the apparent lack of feasibility, should be rejected during this phase.

Phase Three: Feasible Target Solution Development

The purpose of Phase Three is to develop a target learning plan. This is accomplished by collecting the ideas generated during Phase Two into several major categories or groups. These groups of ideas should be directed toward conditions of regularity (i.e., conditions which are the rule, not the exception). Examination of the groups of ideas may be structured to obtain a feasible target plan. This plan may not

Figure 22

Purpose Determination

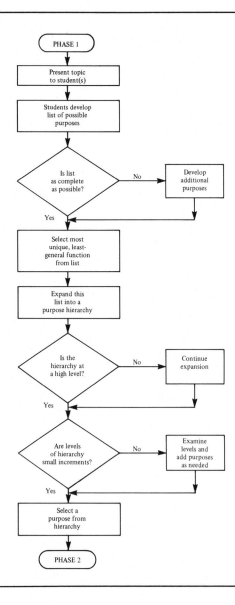

be totally implementable at the present time but will serve as a guide during the subsequent planning efforts. A step-by-step procedure for Phase Three is illustrated schematically in Figure 23.

Phase Four: Detail Recommended Plan

At this stage of the student's design of his or her plan, a feasible target plan has been selected. This plan, however, may not be completely implementable due to resource constraints, such as time, money, personnel, etc. The plan also may not provide for handling certain irregularity conditions and exceptions. The teacher must provide the necessary guidance and direction at this time to assist the student in determining what is practical to consider and what specification of detail is necessary. Specification of detail with respect to system elements (see Figure 13) can be useful during this phase (see Figure 2). Phase Four is shown schematically in Figure 24.

Phase Five: Implementation

Implementation and utilization of the detailed, recommended plan developed in Phase Four are self-explanatory: The student proceeds with the plan he or she developed. However, it is important to remember the iterative and dynamic aspects of the PTR strategy. It may be necessary and/or desirable to review the components defined in the earlier phases. Perhaps the purpose level selected is not appropriate. Certain irregularity conditions may exist which were not considered. Solutions, or possible plans, may arise which were not thought of previously. For whatever reason, there is no reason not to deviate from the recommended plan if conditions suggest this course of action.

Summary

SPARK incorporates a design and planning methodology

Figure 23

Feasible Target Solution Development

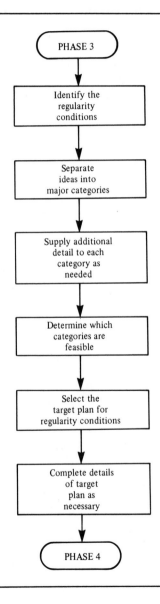

Figure 24

Detail Recommended Plan

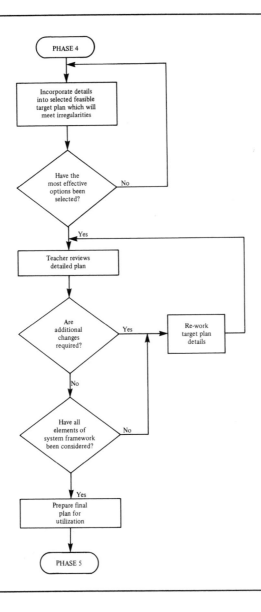

known as the PTR strategy (Purposes-Target-Results). This strategy incorporates five general phases:

(1) purpose determination,

(2) solution generation,

(3) feasible target solution development,

(4) detail recommended plan, and

(5) implementation.

The components of the five phases may be modified according to situational needs. The users should employ them tentatively, constantly examining the plan throughout the design process.

VI.

RESOURCES

BOOKS

Nadler, G. *Work Design: A Systems Concept.* Homewood, Illinois: Richard D. Irwin, Inc., 1970.

Nadler, G. *The Planning and Design Professions: An Operational Theory.* Draft version, University of Wisconsin, Madison, 1979.

Nadler, G., J.T. Johnston, and J.E. Bailey. *Design Concepts for Information Systems.* Atlanta, Georgia: American Institute of Industrial Engineers, 1975.

PAPERS AND REPORTS

Koritzinsky, K.M. (Ed.) KIDS (Kids' Interests Determine Subject). Madison, Wisconsin: Wisconsin Research and Development Center for Cognitive Learning, May 1976.

Nadler, G. Training in a New Strategy for Developing Educational Processes and Products, Document No. SP007897, ED 0901070, *Research in Education,* August 1974.

Nadler, G. A Method of Asking the Right Question, Occasional Paper #12, Phi Delta Kappa Research Service Center, Bloomington, Indiana, 1976.

Nadler, G., and W.J. Gephart. The Process of Development, Occasional Paper #15, Phi Delta Kappa Research Service Center, Bloomington, Indiana, 1974.

Robinson, G.H., and G. Nadler. Curriculum Development with a System Design Strategy, two papers, Department of Industrial Engineering, UW-Madison, Madison, Wisconsin, 1971.

Schultz, J.V., P.W. Struve, and G. Nadler. An Alternative Approach to Systematic Educational Change. Madison, Wisconsin: Wisconsin Research and Development Center for Cognitive Learning, Theory Paper #67, October 1976.

Struve, P.W., and J.V. Schultz. Planning and Managing the IGE/S (Individually Guided Education/Secondary) School. Madison, Wisconsin: Wisconsin Research and Development Center for Cognitive Learning, Theory Paper #65, November 1976.

SLIDES/TAPES

Long Range Planning, Module S7, Center for Human and Community Development, St. John's University, Collegeville, Minnesota, 1977.

SEMINARS AND COURSES

Annual seminar for planning and design professionals. Contact Prof. G. Nadler, University of Wisconsin, 1513 University Ave., Madison, Wisconsin 53706.

MARGARET NORTON was educated in California schools and received her BA and MA in English from UCLA. She began her teaching career in La Jolla Junior High School in Placentia, California, where she became English Department Chairman and Student Body Advisor. She became English Department Chairman and supervisor for the reading component for a state funded project from 1970 to 1972. In 1972, she was one of 25 educators to attend a federally funded Educational Systems Design Workshop at the University of Wisconsin.

WILLIAM C. BOZEMAN is Assistant Professor of educational administration at the University of Iowa. He received his Ph.D. in educational administration from the University of Wisconsin-Madison. While at the latter institution, he worked at the Wisconsin Research and Development Center for Cognitive Learning with the WIS-SIM computer-managed instruction project. In addition to his work at the university level, he has taught high school mathematics and physics, served as federal projects director for a public school district, and has been a high school principal.

GERALD NADLER is Professor of Industrial Engineering (IE) at the University of Wisconsin-Madison. He served as Chairman in 1964-67 and 1971-75. Until June, 1964, he was Professor and Chairman, Department of IE at Washington University in St. Louis, Missouri, where he started as an Assistant Professor in 1949 after receiving the Ph.D. in IE from Purdue University. He is a member of seven professional organizations, in several of which he has served as an officer, and has been on editorial boards for a number of national and international journals.